YOU CAN
MANAGE
YOUR LIFE

YOU CAN MANAGE YOUR LIFE

Don Mallough

BAKER BOOK HOUSE
Grand Rapids, Michigan 49506

Copyright 1981 by
Baker Book House Company

ISBN: 0-8010-6114-8

Printed in the United States of America

Contents

Abbreviations of Bible Translations

AB   *The Amplified Bible.* Copyright 1965 by Zondervan Publishing House.

NEB   *The New English Bible.* Copyright 1961 by The Oxford University Press and The Cambridge University Press.

NIV   *New International Version.* Copyright 1978 by New York International Bible Society.

PHILLIPS   *The New Testament in Modern English.* Copyright 1958 by J. B. Phillips.

It is never too late:

To plan your life
To sharpen your mental faculties
To upgrade your caliber of living
To attain new heights
To plunge into new adventures
To make a fresh start

Preface

Ted found himself in a situation he hadn't antici-
pated. At a PTA meeting he expressed his firm convic-
tions on an issue under discussion. Later he was
appointed to the committee assigned to resolve the
issue. Then the night before the meeting his telephone
rang. The chairman of the committee had been rushed
to the hospital. Ted was asked to take over the leadership. With reluctance, and without thinking it through,
he accepted.

That night Ted was unable to sleep. Emotions were
running high on the issue. Anything could happen.
Some of those hotheads were on the committee, too.
Where, and how, would he begin? What if it all ended
in turmoil? Why, O why, had he allowed himself to get
into this situation?

He thought his wife Alice was asleep until she spoke.
"Ted, shouldn't you have some kind of an agenda for
that meeting? Then you'll know exactly what to do."

Those were the words of wisdom. He drew up a simple agenda for the meeting and let it rest with that. Soon he was asleep. He slept well the night after the meeting, too. The agenda kept the meeting on course, and all went well.

Life need not be a Fibber McGee's closet. If a simple agenda can expedite the work of a committee, it can do even more for a cluttered life. In spite of the buffeting currents of adversity, uncertainty, and changing circumstances, it is possible to enjoy a structured life. The responsibility for bringing order out of disarray rests squarely on your shoulders. Life is what you make it. You alone can produce a pattern of rhyme and reason for your own life.

This is not a book of easy solutions. It does not offer precut, mass-produced molds that will fit every life. The simple premise of this book is that planning is essential, efficiency is possible, and organization is a worthy goal.

In this book I share the experiences of others and the principles emerging from their successes and failures. Let these examples be a challenge to you as you apply them to the appropriate areas of your life.

Don Mallough
Toledo, Washington

1

The Case for Self-Discipline

In the battle of ideas the disciplined mind has an advantage. In the race of life it is the disciplined body that wins. In the arena of living it is the disciplined character that produces the greatest influence for good.

Discipline is a vital element in shaping our lives. Our first experience with discipline is in the home, under the loving guidance of our parents. The structures of the classroom provide further experience with discipline. All such experiences are part of a molding process. This process establishes guidelines and precepts that enable us to cope with the harsh realities of life.

Planning and discipline are key ingredients in the recipe for a happy and productive life. They help one to anticipate and prepare for the future. In that sense they are investments that will pay dividends in days to come. A true disciplinarian does not merely sit back and wait for his paycheck every Friday. He tills the ground and sows the seed with the full expectation that the harvest will inevitably come.

My mother was a language teacher. As a result, I knew her as a teacher as well as a mother. In both areas she was an effective disciplinarian. In fact, there were times when I thought she was too effective. My classmates agreed on that point, and I would bear the brunt of their complaints. I can still hear their complaints. "Whew, your mother is really hard on us. I wish I hadn't taken her class," or "Boy, is she strict! Is she like that at home, too?" There may be advantages to having your mother as a teacher, but I had a strong feeling that it didn't add to my popularity with my fellow students.

Mother is gone now, and many of us are older today than she was in those days. In my travels I often meet old classmates who studied under her. It is interesting to see how they have changed their tune. Some of the same people who used to grumble now say, "You know, I learned more from your mother than from any of my other teachers" or "She made me toe the line, but it was the best thing that ever happened to me."

Your need for discipline still exists today. But who is to administer it at this stage in your life? You are outside the pale of parents and teachers. The responsibility that was once borne by others now rests heavily on your shoulders. No one else can be your disciplinarian now. This is the point when self-discipline must take over and contribute to dynamic living.

Are you in charge of your life, or is it subject to the whims of emotions, appetites, and moods? Is your life organized, or is it disjointed? Is there a structure in your daily routine, or do you just go at things in a hit-or-miss fashion? Do you have a positive plan of action, or do you merely react to the vagaries of circumstances?

The undisciplined life is marked by uncertainty, ambivalence, and vacillation. It is influenced by such minor factors as feelings, opinions of others, hunger, thirst, the sex drive, and even the weather. The undisciplined person follows the whims of these and other factors without exercising any judgment as to which carries the most weight. This leads to a turbulent chaos in which unrestrained influences vie with each other for control of the person's actions. This situation can be likened to a mobocracy, as opposed to the efficient government of the disciplined life.

To bring order into a cluttered life, someone must assume control and give orders. Someone must establish priorities. Someone must set up principles of conduct. The situation calls for a firm hand. For a time, at least, someone must be a veritable dictator.

YOU are that someone! Who else would have the authority to do the job? It is your life to live, and the benefits of self-discipline will accrue to you. No one else has an incentive equal to yours. Others may suggest a plan for your life, but they cannot initiate the plan or make it work. Others may set goals for you, but only you can achieve them. Others may admonish you to finish the projects you start, but you alone can carry through to the end and experience the inner glow of satisfaction that results. For this reason, self-discipline is much more effective than the best training from an outside source.

Self-discipline provides an inner structure that buttresses a person against all the storms and vicissitudes of life. This structure is to the life what the skeleton is to the body. It is a framework of self-imposed rules, principles, and patterns of living. The person with self-discipline not only establishes these precepts but implements them as well.

What are you doing with the only life you have? To what extent are you using the talents that have been entrusted to your care? Are you in control, or are you merely caught in the crosscurrents of what the day may bring?

You are the master of your future. You are at the helm of your life and can choose your destination. You hold the reins of the prancing steed that wants to run wild. How do you measure up to that responsibility?

Now is the time to get tough on yourself. Take charge of your life and demonstrate that you are in control. Dare to discipline and lay down the law. Have the firmness to make decisions and the tenacity to stick to them. Declare war on the shoddy and shabby lifestyle. Meet head-on the tendency to procrastinate. Marshal all your energies to challenge complacency. Harness your limitless potential by planning and organizing your life. Ride herd on the whims and impulses that would deter you from your goals. Exercise the fortitude that enables you to complete every task you undertake. Demonstrate the solid characteristics of constancy and consistency.

Chart a new course for your life!

2

Go Out on a Limb!

Only those who jump into the water learn to swim. The bold and venturesome develop their unused talents, while the cautious hang back. He who never does anything until he feels qualified will accomplish little. The person who fears making a mistake has already made a colossal blunder. Those who brave risks come out on top, while the fearful are haunted by indecision.

There comes a time to break off discussion and make a decision, to stop studying and start doing, to stop hesitating and take action. When bogged down with indecision, do something! Meet the challenge head-on. Snap the chains of timidity. Brave the uncertainties. Scorn the risks. Flout your fears. Go out on a limb!

Commit Yourself to Do Something

Angelo had always wanted to be a teacher. He took all the required courses in high school, and then went on to college. When he received his degree, Angelo decided that he wasn't quite prepared to teach. Without even applying for a job, he went on and spent another year in school. At the end of that year, he decided that he needed one more year to fully prepare. After several years of this, Angelo gave up altogether on the idea of teaching. Although he was more than adequately prepared, he claimed that he would never be qualified. Actually, it was Angelo's acute sense of inadequacy, not his lack of qualifications, that kept him from looking for a job.

No one ever feels adequate to tackle a new job. Those who say they do are merely compensating. If we submit to our feelings at such times, we'll become losers like Angelo.

Clayton has a beautiful voice. He loves music and relishes every opportunity to sing a solo. One year he was asked to lead the singing of Christmas carols at the company party. Had he been asked to sing, he would have jumped at the chance. But this was something different. He had never directed singers before. He would look silly up there waving his arms, especially when he wasn't confident about his ability to keep time. He would most likely make a fool of himself and spoil his image with his fellow employees and the company brass. He ended up making a feeble excuse to avoid the risk of failure.

Then someone mentioned Ed from the accounting department. Ed has a good voice but is not a soloist. He had never led group singing before, but when asked he was ready and eager to give it a try. He goofed a time or two, but that didn't daunt him. Soon everyone was singing lustily, and it was an enjoyable experience for all.

Several years have passed since then. Ed has developed into an excellent songleader and is in great demand to lead group singing. It is an activity that adds zest to his life. Clayton still sings solos but contends that he just doesn't have the ability to lead a community sing.

It is sometimes necessary to force yourself to do something. There may be risks involved, but fear only exaggerates them. The best way to dispel fear is to be aggressive. Become a doer instead of a dreamer. Volunteer for a task and then do your best. Eagerly accept an assignment, whether or not it is in the field of your expertise. Put yourself in a place where you can't back down. Go out on a limb!

Commit Yourself to Do Something Within a Given Time

All of us tend to procrastinate. We have a great backlog of aspirations, but they never seem to get done. Our intentions are the best, but our performance is poor.

One way to galvanize yourself into action is to set a specific deadline for a project. A deadline provides an incentive to act. It goads us to start, continue, and finish a task. It is a form of pressure that changes vague plans into tangible accomplishments.

From early childhood we have been conditioned to work under the pressure of deadlines. Mother said, "You may go out to play when you have finished your homework." The teacher said, "The book report is due on Friday." The boss said, "I'll need that financial report by the time the board meets."

Circumstances often force deadlines upon us. If we are told on Thursday that guests are coming for the weekend, everyone begins to work fast and furiously. Things get done that have been neglected for months. The time limit generates an urgency. Without it, the good intentions are there but the incentive to act is weak.

Self-imposed deadlines are by far the most effective. Why be dependent on the vagaries of circumstance and the dictates of others? Assign yourself a task and a deadline. Are you going to write a family history some day? Set a deadline and start work on it. Finish it by Christmas so that copies can be given to family members. Otherwise it will get lost in the shuffle. Have you always wanted to paint a picture? Use your vacation time and resolve to have the picture finished and framed by the time you get back to your job. Are you going to organize your records? You've said that for years. Go out on a limb and set a deadline. Then make everything else expendable until the task is completed.

Commit Yourself to Do Something in a New Area

Is it good or bad to be a specialist? It all depends on how you view it. Talent, training, and experience have produced many specialists. They are experts in their field, and that is good. But they are often utterly helpless outside the limited sphere of their expertise. That, of course, is bad.

An expert in one field need not be inept in all others. However, if he is plagued by extreme caution and self-deprecation in an unfamiliar field, he will probably be unsuccessful. A remedy for that is to throw caution to the wind and plunge into the new area of activity.

To most people Todd seems to be a reserved, self-conscious man. This all changes, however, when Todd works with boys. He has a rapport with them that is lacking in his relationships with others. He loves boys and boys love him. He has been active in the Boys Club, Boy Scouts, and with the boys in his church.

One day Todd was invited to speak at the Kiwanis Club about his work with boys. Just the thought of speaking to 150 prominent businessmen gave Todd paroxysms of fear. Desperately he searched for an excuse to turn down the invitation, but his wife insisted that he accept. He would be talking about something he loved, she said, and besides, it would be good experience for him. Todd finally consented, but he spent several sleepless nights. When the time finally came for the presentation, however, it went perfectly.

Today Todd is what he never dreamed he could be: a successful public speaker. His contribution to his field is far greater because he is now able to interest and recruit others. And it all happened because he ventured into a new area of activity.

Tom is a lawyer and has a very keen mind. Yet he has always been utterly helpless when it comes to working with his hands. He can't repair the simplest thing around the house. His way of fixing things is to call the repairman.

One cold Saturday morning Tom's doorbell rang. It was Mrs. Swenson, the sweet little old lady from next door. Her water pipes were frozen and she needed "a man" to thaw them. Could Tom help her? His wife Martha overhead the conversation and couldn't believe her ears when she heard Tom say, "I'll be right over as soon as I finish my coffee." Mrs. Swenson thought a man could help her. Could he let her think he was less than a man?

Tom puttered around with the pipes most of the morning. He had no idea what he was doing. Several times he was tempted to call a plumber and pay the bill, but he knew he would lose face that way. Finally, he made a lucky guess and got the water flowing again. Mrs. Swenson thanked him profusely, but that was nothing compared to the great satisfaction he felt at being able to do something no one thought he could do (except Mrs. Swenson, of course).

Would you believe that Tom is now Mrs. Swenson's regular handyman? He even fixes many things around his own home. He is as proud of his mechanical ability as a college graduate is of his diploma. And it all happened because he was pressured into doing something he had never done.

Dare to do something different. Venture into those waters you always thought were too deep. You will be surprised at the results.

Commit Yourself to Do Something
You Can't Do

Most of our limitations are of our own making. If something looks like a challenge, it's easier to say it's impossible and then forget it. This is a form of self-deception. Each time it happens another block is laid in the wall that encircles us.

The greater part of the word *impossible* is *possible.* The same is true in our personal lives. What we term impossible is often possible. Hence, my paradoxical admonition to you: Do what you can't do.

Is there something others can do but you cannot? Is there an area where you are short on ability? Are you lacking in certain talents? If so, it is time for aggressive action. Weak legs are made strong by putting weight on them. Muscles are built by exercise. Amazing discoveries are made by fearless explorers. Opportunities come to those who probe for them.

Go out on a limb! Make a strength out of a weakness. Discover skills that are dormant. Develop abilities where none exist. Venture into a mind-expanding, muscle-strengthening, soul-stretching experience. Learn well the secret expressed by the apostle Paul: "I can do everything through him who gives me strength" (Phil. 4:13, NIV).

3

Goals and Projects

On your journey through life, are you a tramp or a traveler? There is a basic difference between the two. Both words describe individuals who are continually on the move, but there the similarity ends.

A tramp is a nomad who rambles aimlessly. He has a restless spirit and hits the trail just to be traveling. His theme song is, "I don't know where I'm going, but I'm on my way."

A traveler has a fixed destination. Whether or not the trip itself is enjoyable is immaterial. For him travel is a means of reaching a desired place. He knows where he is going, and all his efforts focus on reaching his destination.

The history of the ancient Israelites records a classic example of travelers who degenerated into tramps. For centuries the Israelites had cherished the hope of living in Canaan. God had promised this land to their forefathers, and finally they were enroute from Egypt to that land beyond the Jordan river. Yet, the exodus became a strange anomaly. Having set out eagerly for their future home, they dawdled along the way as if their travels were without purpose. It took the Israelites forty years to traverse an area that could have been covered in forty days. They were constantly moving, but gaining no ground. They played at traveling by merely going in circles.

The Israelites lost sight of their goal. They were glad to have left Egypt with all of its evils and discomforts, but they had forgotten God's purpose in freeing them. The objective of reaching the promised land had long since been forgotten. They began as pilgrims but became mere wanderers who knew only the mechanics of packing and moving.

Suddenly, God jolted them out of their rut of constant circling. He gave Moses, their leader, a rebuke and a command. "You have roamed around this mountain country long enough; turn northward" (Deut. 2:3, AB). In essence He said, "Focus on your goal and march toward it."

The key to growth, success, and happiness lies in having goals and striving toward them. J. C. Penney, who knew men as well as his field of merchandising, once said, "Give me a stock clerk with a goal, and I will give you a man who will make history. Give me a stock clerk without a goal, and I will give you a stock clerk." Earl Nightingale summed it up beautifully when he said, "A person without a goal, toward which he is consciously and daily striving, is like a ship without a rudder, drifting aimlessly at sea."

Setting a goal is the first step toward reaching any

objective. It provides a sense of direction. Keeping the goal in sight makes all the strivings, struggles, and efforts worthwhile. Just knowing where we are going makes other uncertainties fall into place.

Having a goal produces incentive, which is the fuel for resolute action. It also encourages constancy, consistency, and stability. Reaching a goal and moving toward a more difficult one are a means of growth and development. Having a goal is even good medicine. It is the remedy for boredom, which is the root of many physical and mental ailments.

Without goals life is chaotic. Anything can happen when we are subject to every wind, whim, and circumstance. Because we have no sense of direction, the issues confuse us. Our vision is blurred, and we may come to the conclusion that life is a mess. Donald Laird expressed it well when he wrote, "Men and women who go through life without goals . . . are like tired children. They don't know what they want and will not stop whining until they get it."

Nothing is more depressing than to see a once-useful life disintegrate and crumble through a lack of firm inner purpose. Many of us have seen this happen to friends when they entered a critical time of life called retirement. Why is the adjustment from the work-a-day world to the leisure life so devastating for so many persons? Why do the obituaries appear so soon after the retirement party and the gift of the gold watch? Why does the long-anticipated freedom turn into tedium and boredom?

The answer is simple. The inner structure of goals and ambitions has suddenly collapsed. Gone is the framework of responsibility and the structure of the daily work schedule. Any vocational objectives have either been achieved or gone by the board. Even if retirement had been the objective, it is at hand. Without goals to consummate or targets to hit, the meaning and purpose of life is lost. Then come the expressions of disillusionment: "What is the meaning of this kind of life, anyway?" "What good am I now? I'm only a nuisance to others." The malaise of retirement is the result of a complete lack of goals. Why are goals needed at this stage of life? The answer is obvious. Goals are essential in every period of our existence if life is to be meaningful and productive.

An unfortunate circumstance caused my friend Andy to lose his job ten years before he reached retirement age. His health was good, and he began his search for a second career. Day after day he beat the pavement, looking for a job. After a time he would have been satisfied with just any job. Unfortunately nothing was available for a man of his age. Because his wife and children worked and they had a small reserve in savings, Andy did not need a job to stay afloat financially. His family was not perturbed about his vain search, but Andy was. He became morose and miserable, often expressing the feeling that he was a dead weight on his family. He didn't want to meet people because they often embarrassed him by asking questions about his work. He just sat in his big chair and complained about the meaninglessness of his life. The retirement which was thrust on him left him with nothing for which to live. Not too long after the loss of his job, Andy passed away. I don't know what the exact words were on Andy's death certificate, but his doctor said that Andy had just lost the will to live.

Without a doubt, setting goals is vitally important to life and has a profound effect on our sense of well-being. Targets, deadlines, and self-imposed quotas not only constitute a challenge but trigger incentive, provide a sense of direction, emphasize important values, and give zest to life. Then when a goal is reached, the gratifying sense of accomplishment puts the icing on the cake.

Here are a few helpful suggestions for setting goals: Fix your aspirations, review them often, and rejoice when they are reached. Soon structured living will become so important that you will never revert to a slipshod lifestyle.

Set Specific Goals

Think and express yourself in precise terms. Pinpoint exactly what you want to accomplish. The more you spell out the details, the easier it will be to focus on your objective. You will also know when you have reached your goal and can revel in the flush of achievement.

If your goal is to increase your vocabulary, tell yourself, "I'm going to add 150 words to my vocabulary within this year." This establishes a precise target. You could say, "I'm going to improve my communication skills." But this goal is fuzzy and imprecise. It is obviously easier to accomplish the more detailed objective.

There are little secrets to psyching yourself. One

way is to express your goal in writing. Paste it on your bathroom mirror or in any place where you will see it often. Another way to motivate yourself is to periodically review your progress. In the case of learning new words, have a numbered list and keep tabs on how many you have learned and how many you have to go. Tell your spouse and others close to you of your goal. Because they believe in you, they will be pulling for you and would be disappointed if you fell short.

Set Demanding Goals

In order to justify its very existence and fulfill its purpose, a goal must make the utmost demands. Anything less and it would cease to be a goal. Don't con yourself into thinking that routine accomplishments and ordinary mileposts can be called goals. That which comes easily and is performed without effort is merely the routine.

A goal must be difficult enough to provide a challenge, to stretch our capability and capacity, and to make demands on all of our resources. A goal must be demanding enough to bring faith into play.

Set Achievable Goals

A goal can be both difficult and achievable. If a goal is unreachable, it does not necessarily mean it is too difficult, although that is possible. It would be foolish for me to set a goal to be the first man to climb Mount Everest. The little word *first* makes this an unattainable goal. Sir Edmund Hillary has beaten me to it. The same would be true if I substituted the word *only.* I have no control over whether others reach the peak or not. I can, however, have a legitimate goal to climb the highest mountain in the world.

A small church displayed a bulletin board that said:

Sunday School Attendance

TODAY—87   RECORD—103   GOAL—1,000

This Sunday school was to be commended for having a goal, but I fear their choice was a poor one. The gap between where they were and where they aspired to be was so wide as to be discouraging rather than challenging. The church itself would not seat over 300 and the Sunday school facilities would accommodate less than that. An achievable and realistic goal, without an enlared building, would be 275. Such a goal for them would be reachable—and could always be raised as the attendance increased and new facilities were provided.

The impetus in a well-ordered life stems from setting goals, but the joy comes when goals are realized. The secret is in keeping a balance between the two. The process of establishing goals, reaching them, and then raising our sights and stretching our ambitions toward even greater heights results in personal growth and happiness.

Set Lifelong Goals

An important piece of equipment in the cockpit of the huge airliners is the automatic pilot. The automatic pilot keeps the plane on course. Long-range goals in a life serve in a similar capacity.

Lifetime goals may be few, but they are vitally important. To get them into focus, just ask yourself three simple questions. What do I want to possess in life? What do I want to do vocationally? What do I want to be as a person? Spell out the answers clearly and concisely. These are your goals. Do more than just write them down, however. Now that you know where you want to go, get a fix on each target. Ponder each one until your goals not only fill your thoughts but become deeply etched in your subconscious mind. When they are deeply ingrained there, they will be a guiding influence regardless of your momentary thoughts or capricious actions. When a circumstance throws you temporarily off course, your subconscious mind will recognize the inconsistency with your established objectives in life and slowly bring you back on course. Your automatic pilot is adjusted to the goals you have chosen. What you want to be, you will be.

Set Short-term Goals

When I was in my early twenties I stumbled on a reference book that proved to be a gold mine. With diligent application it could provide a valuable education. I was so enthusiastic I had to share it with my friend Artie, who was a lover of good books.

"That's great, Don," he exclaimed. "It will be of tremendous value to you. I only wish something like that was available when I was younger. It's rather late for me now at forty-two years of age."

The too-late syndrome is the arch-enemy of ambition. It is the swamp in which the fungus of self-pity thrives. It makes invalids of persons when their bodies are still hale and hearty.

A study was made of four hundred outstanding achievers. The names were chosen from a wide variety of vocations and activities. Experts were asked to review, evaluate, and amend the selections.

It was found that persons between the ages of sixty and seventy produced thirty-five percent of the world's great achievements. Twenty-three percent were produced by persons between seventy and eighty years of age. The most outstanding finding of this study was that sixty-four percent of the great achievements were made by persons who had passed their sixtieth birthday. Obviously each accomplishment sprang from a fixed goal in the heart of that person.

There is no period in life when goals are unnecessary. Even if threatened by actuarial tables, put out to pasture by our peers, or surrounded by doddering friends, we have a life to live—and to the fullest degree. Doing so involves both aspirations and achievements. Setting goals is an integral part of any accomplishment and a contributor to dynamic living, whatever the milepost along the pathway. Goals are goals, whether long-range or short-term. Making good use of both types will bring you an energetic and exuberant life.

This is, as the popular saying goes, the first day of the rest of your life. No matter how many birthdays lie behind you, it is the time that is ahead that counts. You will not achieve any more in your future than the goals you establish right now. It may be too late to set a vocational goal, but there are still many things for you to do. Challenge yourself, stretch your faith, and enlarge your vision. This is the day for action. And action begins by establishing goals.

Get Involved in Projects

A project is second cousin to a goal. There is a close relationship, and yet they are different. A project is an undertaking or enterprise requiring concerted effort. It is not just an ordinary job but something to stimulate enthusiasm. Generally a goal is in the future, while a project requires immediate planning, participation, and work.

On one occasion I was shocked to hear a successful pastor say, "I never allow any church I serve to be out of debt. When one mortgage is burned we plunge into something else." Had he expressed himself differently, no eyebrows would have been raised. He could have said, "I never allow any church I serve to be without a project." It was his philosophy that it is unhealthy for a congregation to be without a challenge. In that he was absolutely right. Neither should an individual be without a challenging and stimulating project. The happiest persons are those who are involved in such ventures.

When I called on Martha she was eighty-eight years old and living alone. Bubbling with enthusiasm, she told me of all that she was doing. She was deeply involved in writing poetry, music, and prose. She had several chapters of a family history completed, which, she assured me, wasn't for publication but for her son. She practiced scales on her piano to keep her fingers limber. She was compiling a cookbook and planning to take a ceramics class.

"There are so many interesting things to do," she exulted, "that my problem is finding time to do them."

There was no reason to feel sorry for Martha. She was living life to the fullest. Her secret was that she was immersed in her projects and reveled in them.

The joy of retirement is that it is a release from an oppressive work schedule. There is no ringing alarm, no hectic rush to punch the time clock, and no imposed regimen of activity. Work is not banned, however. The retired person can work hard if he desires and quit when the task becomes burdensome. Instead of work being thrust on him by others, it is done of his own volition. He does what he wants to do when he wants to do it.

Your goals and your projects must be born in your heart. Anything imposed by others will soon become a galling yoke. No one else can make the vital decisions that will determine your future. Even your closest friends may not agree with the objectives you choose. It is your life to live. It is your happiness that is at stake.

4

Getting Things Done

The true gauge of success in life is not how long or hard we work but what we get accomplished. The busiest persons are not always the most productive. "Busy-ness" is not necessarily business. Some persons merely pretend to be busy for a studied effect. Others make a sincere effort but accomplish little. Both types are frustrating themselves and frittering away the essence of life—time.

To get bogged down in an objectionable chore is disheartening. The inefficiency which prolongs that experience may seem to be unavoidable. However, inefficiency can be remedied by removing distractions and developing a suitable plan of action.

Few experiences are more exhilarating than a provocative challenge. Even more rewarding, however, is the sense of accomplishment that we feel when we have met the challenge and a difficult task has been completed. When we increase our efficiency, we also increase our opportunities to meet new challenges, and gain new victories.

Successful persons in all walks of life have learned a few simple secrets for getting things done. Some have learned the hard way, through the frustrating experience of trial and error. Others have been wise enough to learn by observing those who get results and by listening to their suggestions and advice.

Following are six basic secrets that will make your busy day more meaningful and help you to get more results for your efforts.

Plan Your Day

The first step is to spell out what you hope to accomplish. A good way to do this is to allow yourself a few minutes each day to list your most pressing duties. Anticipating your tasks and writing them down will help to crystallize them in your mind. In the process you will be setting a quota for yourself. It is better to plan too much than too little. If a task is not accomplished, put it on the list for the next day. If practical, make it the first item. That way it will not be lost in the shuffle and become expendable.

Organize Your Work

When you outline your tasks for the day, attempt to arrange them in a logical sequence. Some matters will take priority because of deadlines or importance. Put first things first on the schedule. When it becomes habitual to systematize your work in this way, you will wonder how you got along on the hit-or-miss method.

Break Down the Complicated Jobs

We avoid some tasks because they seem too difficult. A secret in handling difficult jobs is to separate them into logical parts and take care of one part at a time until the entire job is done. Bite off only that part which you can chew. If you keep at it steadily, you will be surprised at how much you can devour.

Because my work requires travel I have found it necessary to do much of my heavy reading on a rigorous schedule. For example, I may decide to read a particular book during an engagement. I squeeze the book into my luggage, knowing it will be there for only that one trip. I give myself a high priority assignment to read a certain number of pages each day. By the end of the trip I have read the book, taken notes, and mailed it home or given it to someone else to enjoy. In addition to completing the book, there is the added incentive of lightening my luggage.

Take on the Hardest Job First

Putting off a hard job makes it even more difficult. Gear your mental attitude to do the hardest job early in the morning. Once you have completed it, a sense of satisfaction will prevail through the remainder of the day.

Stay with Your Schedule

Since you have drawn up your own work schedule, you can break it if you desire. No one will reprimand you for doing so. If that is your decision, however, you are defeating your own purpose. You organized your work in the interests of getting more done. If that is still your aim, then you should follow your schedule as though a strict disciplinarian were imposing it on you. Emergencies will arise to interrupt, but if you abide by the schedule most of the time, you will soon form work habits that will become second nature.

Report Back to Yourself

When an executive delegates responsibility to one of his staff, he expects a report on completion of the task. When you assign a job to yourself, it is only logical that you report back to yourself. This will give you a sense of achievement and create an incentive to do even more.

The simplest method of reporting is to check off the items on your list of jobs. The knowledge that you are going to do this will spur you to fulfill all the tasks you have scheduled.

In addition to these six secrets for getting things done, there are three pitfalls that must be avoided. They are well camouflaged, but any one of them will sabotage your whole program. Unless you avoid them, your good work habits will be for naught.

Avoid Distractions

While you are concentrating on an important task, be assured that other interests will bid for your attention. If you are doing research, there will be the temptation to wander on an attractive path and forget the object of your study. If you are doing a tedious physical job, the siren song will subtly beckon you to duties that are far less strenuous. It is amazing how prolific the human mind is at thinking of other things to do when facing a formidable task. The temptation is not to do what is wrong but to do the right thing at the wrong time.

When you are engaged in one job, it is no time to wander off in many directions. The first thing to realize is that the detour is not a pleasant by-path upon which to meander but a deceptive distraction leading away from your goal. The person who yields to the temptation to wander off on tangents will be frustrated in his accomplishments. To get more done, we must concentrate on the work we have set out to do.

"What do you plan to do today?" a farmer's wife asked him at breakfast.

"I must take advantage of the good weather," he replied, "and get that last thirty acres plowed."

While he was lubricating the tractor, he ran out of grease. As he walked to his shop to get more, he saw his old truck, which reminded him that one of the tires had a slow leak. It took only half an hour to change it. As he passed the woodpile he remembered his wife needed some kindling. After that, he took a few minutes to catch up on the local news in the weekly paper.

Finally ready to get to the plowing, he headed toward the machine shed. A banging noise caught his attention.

The corncrib door was hanging nearly off its hinges. He had it fixed by the time lunch was ready.

The rest of the day went by in the same way. The potatoes had to be put in the cellar, the fence mended, and the chickens fed. By late afternoon the snow had begun to blow. As he washed up for the evening meal, he remarked, "Everything ganged up on me today. What a shame that I didn't get the plowing done."

Avoid Procrastination

Putting off any job magnifies its difficulties. With each passing day it becomes more of an insurmountable barrier. Dreading a task can be more tiring than doing it. The person who habitually procrastinates only makes himself miserable.

Try a simple experiment. Think of a phone call you should make. Put it off until tomorrow. Then think about it again, but postpone it for another day. Before long you will have developed such a dread about the call that you will make every effort to avoid making it.

Even the slightest duty is a potential problem when it is deferred. The longer the delay, the more complicated the task becomes. When several tasks are delayed, the difficulty is greatly multiplied. A logjam develops and only dynamite can break it up. Temporizing can become a vicious habit, one that will make a person his own worst enemy.

Avoid the Nonessential Tasks

Every person has favorite types of work. Because the work is fascinating to him, he must fight the tendency to devote too much time to it.

I have a minister friend who has a flair for art work. He spends hours with pen, pencil, and stylus, sketching artistic designs and curlicues for the church bulletin. He has assumed the role of chief signpainter and producer of all posters for the bulletin board. He creates masterpieces—while his secretary has to scratch to keep busy. He has a great talent for such activity, but he neglects more important matters.

Then there is the busy executive who is a self-appointed travel agent. He is a globetrotter and likes nothing better than to be surrounded by atlases, timetables, and travel folders, planning a trip to some remote area. The work that a travel agency would gladly do he takes on himself because he so thoroughly enjoys it. If he hears of someone who is anticipating a trip, he volunteers to work out all of the details. He does a superb job, but his preoccupation with his hobby tends to sabotage the important work he should be doing.

Now is the time to evaluate your work/accomplishment ratio. Are you working hard but not getting much done? If you will carefully put into practice these six simple secrets and avoid the three pitfalls, you will be delighted with the results. The inner glow that comes with having successfully completed a task will be yours at the end of every day.

5

Decisions and Priorities

A farmer hired a young man to help around the farm. The lad proved to be as fast a worker as the farmer had ever seen. Time after time he finished his tasks with remarkable speed.

One morning the farmer told the youth to go the root cellar and sort potatoes. He was to separate the potatoes into three piles: the best ones for eating, the smaller ones for seed, and the damaged ones for feeding the hogs. The day wore on and the farmer saw nothing of his helper. Finally he went to the cellar, where he found the lad sitting on the floor with potatoes scattered all around him. When he asked if something was wrong, the young man replied, "I don't mind the work, but these decisions are killing me!"

The ability to make decisions ranks high among the qualifications for success. It is the distinctive mark of an achiever. Top executives are paid for their skill in making and implementing decisions. Astute statesmen have the uncanny faculty for rejecting the impractical, eliminating the extraneous, and making decisions that influence the course of history. The decisions of these pacesetters are not always right, but enough of them are correct to keep things moving. Every accomplishment starts with a decision. Hence, a doer must be a decision maker.

Making decisions is one of the most important, demanding, exciting, and rewarding activities of life. A decision makes things happen. It breaks ground for important events. It gives birth to a squalling baby of great potential.

The process of making a decision is often the most difficult part of any task. It is a ravenous consumer of energy and strength. The rough and tumble of mental wrestling is exhausting. But the gratification that one feels when a decision is final and a project is launched makes the effort worthwhile.

Indecision is an agonizing affliction that can easily become a habit. It grows like a fungus. A pattern develops which produces a host of deferred problems cooking on the back burner. Solving problems is rewarding, but merely grappling with difficult issues generates only frustration.

An indecisive person accomplishes little. He comes to a breakthrough and allows it to become a barrier. This type of person also punishes himself. Deferring a decision only compounds the problem and prolongs the anguish. He goes through constant labor pains without the joy of giving birth. The indecisive person deceives himself. He assumes that delay will make the decision easier. Nothing could be farther from the truth.

Indecision is inaction; it is sheer procrastination. Delay makes the obstacles more formidable and the solution more obscure.

When a person does not make a decision, he has already made the wrong one. He has made a decision to do nothing—and it is a decision. Any of the other decisions would be better than to pretend he has avoided making one.

One of the colorful idioms of our language is the phrase "passing the buck." It is a shortened form of "passing the buckhorn knife." It means to shift responsibility or blame to someone else. During his tenure in the White House, President Harry S. Truman had a motto on his desk, saying, "The Buck Stops Here." Great leaders are acutely aware that passing the buck is a luxury they no longer possess. The final decision rests with them. An executive must make decisions. The higher and more responsible the position, the more weighty the decisions.

Pope John XXIII told how this fact confronted him: "I often lie awake at night and think about a serious problem and decide I must tell the pope about it. Then I wake up completely and realize that I am the pope."

Setting Priorities

One aspect of making a decision is the setting of priorities. This is a mental process by which problems, tasks, and undertakings are aligned in sequence according to their importance or urgency. Through this process a plan of attack is established. A system is set up to deal with critical matters that are all screaming for attention.

Problems, obligations, and debts have a way of ganging up on us. They come in swarms and attack from all sides like infuriated hornets. All too often we react in a confused frenzy as if we were actually fighting hornets.

The key to solving problems, doing complicated jobs, and paying debts is to set priorities. Decide which one is most important and urgent. Line them up in single file with the most pressing one first. Then deal with them one by one.

Making Decisions

Problems and difficulties are an integral part of living. Only the dead are exempt from them. With the proper attitude and approach, we can make them opportunities in disguise and steppingstones to success.

It is not helpful merely to rehash the basics of a problem. Such contemplation, without taking action, only magnifies the dilemma. One who thoroughly ponders the matter and still cannot make a decision is severely handicapped.

How, then, can one break the exasperating habit of indecision? The first step is to recognize it for what it is—a debilitating, destructive weakness of character. Do not excuse or rationalize this weakness as the trait of a thorough thinker. Do not fool yourself into thinking of it as a commendable virtue of caution. Indecision is a bad habit that has become a rut.

The only way to counteract indecision is to make

decisions. It is as simple as that. Make a decision! It may be the right one, or it may not be. Whatever the choice, it is better than the miseries of indecision. You may make faulty decisions, but who doesn't? One thing is certain. Your batting average cannot help but be higher than it has been, and, more importantly, you will have greater peace of mind.

Every day we are faced with minor decisions. Occasionally a gigantic one will confront us. Don't wait for that big one to break the habit of indecision. Start with the small ones. Break the habit of being indecisive by forming the habit of being decisive.

Face up to your problems. Make firm decisions. Translate the decisions into actions. Be decisive even in changing your mind.

6

Start Vigorously

Getting started is the hardest part of any task. Just getting under way in the morning is an ordeal for many persons. That is why Monday morning is an exceptionally difficult time. It is the start of the work-week. I can fully understand the difficulty of getting started after what happened to my wife and me a few years ago.

Our new house had just been completed, and all our possessions were transported with a rented truck and the help of some friends. Because of the battle with time and darkness, everything was just unloaded in the house. Only one piece of furniture was in its proper place—the bed. There would be another day to arrange everything.

The next morning my wife and I awakened early and were eager to begin arranging our new home. When I opened the bedroom door, my eyes fell on a mountain of junk—a horrendous mess. Where would we even begin to bring order out of such chaos? We made a quick decision and acted on it. We closed the door, piled into bed, and slept half the day away.

The vast majority of us must own up to being slow starters. It is a problem for which there is no outside help. A doctor cannot write a prescription for the disease of dawdling or the disconcerting habit of puttering. We must recognize it as a timewaster that rears its ugly head just when we are about to do something important and productive. It strikes when time is exceedingly valuable.

Charlie is a door-to-door salesman and wouldn't change jobs with anyone. However, a problem has plagued him throughout his career. When ten o'clock comes and it is time to start his rounds, he is beset by qualms and fears. He thinks and behaves like a novice. The first house on the block just doesn't look right to him. Then he goes to the next one and decides that it, too, is not quite right. After several feeble attempts he musters up courage and makes his first call. Then the ice is broken, and Charlie is his normal, ebullient self again—whether or not the call resulted in a sale. He has often said, "I would be all right if I could only transfer the excess enthusiasm I have at the end of the day to my starting time the next morning."

Beginning writers are notorious dawdlers, and some of them never outgrow that pernicious practice. They lean heavily on inspiration when it is writing time. Distractions become attractive, obstacles loom large, and excuses proliferate like rabbits. They sharpen pencils, shuffle papers, straighten up the desk, empty the wastebasket, anything to avoid the hard work of writing.

A would-be writer once proudly told Sir Winston Churchill that unless he had a sudden bolt of inspiration, or was in the mood, he could not write.

"No!" Churchill vehemently replied, "Shut yourself in your study from nine to one and just force yourself to write. Prod yourself! Kick yourself! It is the only way."

Outward appearances are often misleading. If one is hesitant to begin a job, it would seem evident that he is avoiding a dull and distasteful chore. There are times when that is true, but not always. Slow starts also occur when enjoyable activities are involved.

It is contrary to reason that Charlie should stall and waver every morning instead of getting on with the business of making calls. Selling is the joy of his life. Yet he dreads buckling down to what he relishes greatly.

Why should one who lives, breathes, and dreams creative writing allow the sickness of procrastination to cause him to postpone, putter, and make excuses? It doesn't make sense. Yet it happens consistently.

You are not a rare breed if you have trouble getting started. You are just an average person who has a very common problem. Of course, the problem is more extreme with some than with others. The achievers are those who have learned to do something about their problem. The handicapped are those who accept it as inevitable.

The slow start is basically procrastination. It is a subtle habit that masquerades as an incurable affliction.

James Albery wanted to be a writer. He did pen one

memorable verse that expressed a keen sense of self-evaluation. This verse is etched on his tombstone:

> He slept beneath the moon,
> He basked beneath the sun;
> He lived a life of going-to-do,
> And died with nothing done.

How is one transformed from a poky starter to a forceful one? The first step is to recognize the slow start as a problem. Just because it is a common affliction is no excuse to tolerate it. It may be a natural trait, but that is no reason it cannot be changed. However, there must be an intense desire for change before any recasting of a lifestyle is possible. Just a wish expressed in words is not enough.

All action begins with a thought. Mental activity precedes physical exploits. The greatest of human achievements originated with a single, simple idea. Getting started demands resolute thinking and aggressive action.

If you are Charlie, the salesman, then start your day boldly. Take a tip from the athletes. Psych yourself up and make a strength of your weakness. Don't let that first house intimidate you. Don't allow morning cowardice to rob you of even one prospective sale. Push the doorbell eagerly and make your best pitch when the door opens. Whether or not you make a sale, you will be a winner because you have set a positive tone for your whole day.

Another way to whip the swamp-turtle start is to set a specific time to undertake a task. Instead of "I'll do it tomorrow," say "I'll start at 9:32." Then you have a target at which to shoot. The deadline may be of your own making, but it will help you to get started. Anything that does that is worthwhile.

Decisive, vigorous action will shatter the poky-start syndrome. You alone can initiate and implement that action. Assert your leadership. Crack the whip. Get tough and bark out crisp orders to yourself. Break the chains of inertia. Forget the obstacles and get going. Come to grips with the task at hand. Dispel the lethargy and daydreaming.

Don't just mull over the situation—do something about it. Don't dangle your toe in the water—plunge in. Don't merely idle your motor—take off. Don't cater to your feelings—dictate to them.

With a vigorous start you are over the hump, and you can expect great results to follow.

7

Habit and Momentum

Habit

Man is a creature of habit. Chalk that up as a cardinal virtue. In spite of what many people think, habit is not an enemy but a friend. It is not a liability but a priceless asset. To shape our lives by the force of habit is a God-given ability. It is a faculty to cherish and use intelligently.

Many people are hung up on the word *habit*. To them it is always coupled with the word *bad*. They assume that habit itself is evil and to be avoided. Such connotations often stem from past experiences. Perhaps they have experienced the vicelike grip of an unmanageable habit. Or they may have had friends who secumbed to an enslaving addiction. Such experiences naturally color, and tend to limit, the meaning of the word.

Like so many other things in life, habit is neither good nor bad in itself. It depends on how it is used. If we are continually trying to break fixed habits, and finding it difficult, we will naturally think of a habit as something bad. If we are establishing patterns of behavior to enhance our daily living, then we will count habit as an ally.

Within each of us is a robot named habit. It is our servant and is subject to our direction and training. Once the robot is trained, it carries on without conscious instructions from us. Then what is habitual becomes second nature. The secret is to be aware that habit is our servant and not our master.

For the past fifteen years I have started my day by running two miles. I am continually asked, "How do you do it?" My usual reply sounds flippant but is basically true. "Oh, it comes just as naturally as brushing my teeth."

In my boyhood it was a chore to brush my teeth. I would dread it, avoid it, and forget it. Were it not for my mother's continual harping at me, there is no telling what would have happened to my teeth. Now I cannot understand why it was such a problem. The robot of habit has taken over, and I brush my teeth without even thinking about it. So it is with my habit of running each morning.

I have a dear friend who is a minister. For many years he served as an administrative officer at the headquarters of a religious denomination. He was in great demand as a speaker and traversed the nation on speaking engagements. No matter how weary he was from traveling or how late he got home during the night, he was always in church on Sunday morning. The same was true in the evening service.

I could not help but respect his faithfulness, and one day I broached the subject to him.

"Bob, why do you punish yourself that way? You are in church when you've only had three hours sleep. You attend the Sunday night service when you've been preaching the five previous nights and have a heavy work schedule at the office for the next day. No one expects you to do that, not even the Lord."

"I'm well aware of your point, Don," he replied, "and you don't know how tempted I have been to stay in bed instead of going to church. However, here is my reasoning on the matter. We are rearing three boys. I want them to be in church and can't expect them to be if I am home and don't attend church myself." Then came the statement that has etched itself into my memory. "You see, I don't want the time to come in my home when the question is raised, 'Are we going to church today?' I want it to be so natural for all of us to attend that no one will even think of that question."

Perhaps the purest motive for attending church is not mere habit, but the force of habit surely provides a strengthening hand.

All too often we underestimate the value of good habits. The fact that they are operative in our lives is either accidental or incidental. No thought is given, nor effort extended, to develop them. The habits that exist, whether good or bad, stem from a hit-or-miss, nonchalant lifestyle in which we merely accept things as they are. We submit to what happens instead of making things happen. In doing so we lose the services of a good right-hand man—the robot of habit.

A productive life is an efficient life. An efficient life

is an organized life. An organized life is a habit-filled life. Each of these factors contribute to health, happiness, and well-being. William James once said, "There is no more miserable human being than the one with whom nothing is habitual but indecision." When the programmed robot of habit takes over, it relieves us of making many routine decisions, releasing our mental faculties to work in other areas.

We tend to gravitate into bad habits. The good ones are fashioned with conscious forethought and concentrated effort. The technique for establishing good habits involves planned repetition. We spin a gossamer thread that eventually becomes a sturdy cable. Then the actions that were once difficult become second nature. That is when the robot takes over and the force of habit serves its most useful purpose.

Who can compute the power of ingrained habit? The person enslaved by a devastating addiction knows only that it is too much for him. One who is tugged to and fro by ever-changing habit patterns recognizes a potent force but is unable to harness it. The key role of habit was expressed long ago in these words:

> Sow a thought, and you reap an act;
> Sow and act, and you reap a habit;
> Sow a habit, and you reap a character;
> Sow a character, and you reap a destiny.

Habits are an integral part of the pattern of life. We cannot be without them. We can, however, choose which habits will prevail. We can initiate a constructive habit that will eliminate a destructive one. We can make our habits our servants instead of our masters. Specific planning and structured living can put disorder and uncertainty to flight.

Is there a worthy activity that would enrich your daily lifestyle? Perhaps it is something interesting, challenging, or invigorating. I dare you to start this activity, nurture it, cultivate it, and develop it into a habit. The habit you make will help make you.

Momentum

Momentum is another potent force at our disposal. We can latch on to this outside energy source and use it to our advantage. The secret is to recognize its values, sense its existence, and maintain it.

There are several scientific explanations of momentum. For our purpose we need to know just one simple fact. Momentum is the power of a moving body to overcome resistance.

Some years ago I was reminded of the value of momentum. I was seeding a new lawn and had rented a roller to complete the leveling process. I filled the roller with water, to provide the necessary weight, and was ready to go. But I couldn't even budge the clumsy thing. For a moment I thought of giving up. Then I hailed a neighbor, and with his 180 pounds added to my 230 we got it rolling. I thanked him and carried on alone. I knew I had a tiger by the tail, however. If I stopped I would be stalled again. The faster I went, the easier it was. I must have been a sight to behold. I was pushing the heavy roller at racehorse pace, rounding the corners recklessly and as eager to get the job done as if I were fighting fire. I accomplished a formidable task by taking advantage of momentum.

If you had a choice of working with or against the force of gravity, which would you choose? Which makes greater demands on your strength, running uphill or down? Which is easier, rowing upstream or with the current?

The pull of gravity and the force of momentum are very similar. The main difference is that one draws downward and the other thrusts forward. Either one can work for us or against us. These and other outside powers can be used to augment your own efforts.

Momentum is vitally important in the world of competitive sports. It is a key ingredient in the strategy of team sports. Both teams know that the tide can change suddenly. When the momentum swings from one team to another, it changes the fortunes of both.

When driving after a fresh snowfall, it is essential to keep moving. If the car stops it is stuck. That principle prevails in any venture.

Momentum is not constant but sporadic. The secret is to commandeer any existing impetus and hitch a ride. You must be an opportunist and utilize any forward movement to propel you even further. When the adrenalin is flowing is no time to rest. When inspiration flares, forget about going fishing. When enthusiasm is at fever pitch, it is a reproach to sit and whittle. When fresh ideas tumble over each other, it is a crime to turn them off like a tap and go on a picnic.

When the wheels are rolling, jump on board. Momentum is your friend. Maintain it and it will serve you well.

8

Plan Ahead

Planning is a cardinal element in an organized life. Not only is it beneficial to plan, but it is highly important how and when we do so.

Planning is mental spadework that precedes action. But just how far ahead should we plan?

I know two brothers who are clergymen. Each serves a large and influential church. In many ways they are alike. In at least one way they are different.

One spends all day Saturday and even into the wee hours of the morning preparing his Sunday sermon. The other one spends only an hour on Saturday evening reviewing the sermon which was prepared the previous Saturday. He always works a week in advance. The lack of pressure, he feels, allows him to do better work. Both brothers prepare thoroughly, but they differ on how far in advance their preparation is done.

There are deadlines and there are *deadlines,* as any editor knows. There is the absolute one, dictated by events on the schedule, and the arbitrary one, set up in advance to provide a buffer period.

Planning is as helpful in the less important activities of life as it is in the important ones. It conserves time instead of consuming it. It produces efficiency and thoroughness, which are assets in any endeavor.

Travel Plans

Travel is often grueling and demanding, but advance planning makes it easier and more enjoyable. Perhaps a few of my experiences in this area will illustrate how planning can take the frustration out of your travels.

Packing is one of the big problems in traveling. Some people never get the knack of it. The novice packs more clothes for a week than he needs for a month, and then wishes he had brought something else. You can spot him in a moment as he struggles with several heavy bags.

I have found a secret that helps me travel light and yet have all the clothes I need. Before leaving home I make decisions as to what I will wear each day. At a five-day convention I will need five changes of apparel, plus one for travel. At home I pick my outfit for Tuesday: jacket, trousers, shirt, tie, belt, socks, and shoes. I list that information on a small card which eventually goes into my wallet. I do the same for every other day I am to be gone. Then I make a list of all items to be packed. I work from this list when packing my bag and check off each item as it goes in. I don't even take an extra tie.

The only additional effort in this method is making

the list, and that is minimal. Decisions as to what to wear are ordinarily made every morning. I choose to make them before leaving home to avoid carrying needless items and cluttering up my baggage. Planning does not create problems but solves them.

Have you ever been on an extended trip with a car overflowing with people and luggage? What happens when you arrive at a motel for the night? Invariably the bag someone wants most is at the back of the trunk. Mary wants to change shoes. In which bag are they? The hair curlers are somewhere in all that mess, but just where no one knows. The upshot is that most of the baggage must be unloaded and then packed again the next morning.

Surely there is a way to remedy this situation. The ideal is to put all items that will be needed on an overnight stop in one bag. If that is impossible, those that will be needed can be packed so as to be accessible. A list can indicate even where they are. Forethought and planning smooth the path for the traveler.

My wife and I traversed this continent during World War II. We usually traveled by train, an experience that proved to be an education in planning.

The whole nation was on the move, and to us it seemed as if they were all on the trains. Reservations were hard to get, seats were at a premium, coaches were packed, and the stations were a seething mass of humanity. Those in military uniform and the physically handicapped had priority. For others it was a mad scramble and tempers were often short.

Once we were in Oklahoma City, and our next engagement was in Phoenix. There was only one pullman car going to Phoenix, and the reservations had gone so fast that I wasn't able to get one. That meant we would be forced to ride in the coach all night, and there was a possibility that we would have to sit on our luggage or even stand. I had to devise a way to assure that we would at least have a seat.

On Saturday, before we were to depart on Monday, a friend called and asked if I would like to take a ride with him into the country. I expressed delight with the invitation. I explained, however, that first I had to go to the Union Station. He volunteered to drive me there.

At the station I wanted to obtain certain facts. How long before the train's arrival did the passengers start gathering? Did they line up at a station gate, or did they have direct access to the train platform? Just where would the train stop, and where would the Phoenix coach be? I surveyed the whole scene, asked questions, and got the information I needed. Then we went for an enjoyable drive in the country.

On Monday we were among the first passengers to arrive. We went directly to the platform, and I put my bags down at the very spot I had previously surveyed. As others arrived they gathered in clusters, some far ahead of us and others to the rear. We were standing alone. When the train braked to a stop, we were directly in front of a coach door. The conductor opened the door and put down his little stool.

"Destination, please," he said.

"Phoenix."

"This is the car. Watch your step."

Others rushed, scrambled, and hassled, but our seats

were there as if they had been reserved. It was a matter of being in the right place at the right time. We had reclining seats in which to spend the night. That wasn't as good as a berth but better than sitting on bags in the vestibule. Planning made the difference.

Early planning pays off in many ways. I attend some conventions where the type and location of my accommodations are very important. When 15,000 people converge on a city, there is a scramble for rooms and services. I personally investigate the available accommodations and then make my reservations nine months or a year in advance. Should there be a change of plans I can always cancel. That is also true of plane reservations. Why not anticipate your needs and plan for them?

Plane fares between any two cities of the world are not identical. There are so many variations that even travel agencies cannot keep up with them. The general rule is that the lower the fare the more the restrictions. These restrictions may mean that the flight must depart on slow days and not on the weekend. The minimum and maximum duration of the stay may also be specified. On the lowest fares reservations must be made and the tickets purchased a month before departure, and there are penalties for cancellation.

Early planning is just as effective in traveling as in any other activity. It is a means of scouting the trail ahead. Anticipating the difficulties does much to smooth the rocky path. Nothing can instill more confidence than knowing what to expect and how to cope with it.

You have an innate ability to plan. If you have neglected this ability, now is the time to cultivate and nurture it. Planning is an investment in the future. Plant the seed and expect to reap the harvest.

Contingency Plans

In times of war or peace military strategists in the Pentagon are drafting battle plans. In their vast files of contingency plans are detailed procedures for any conceivable circumstance that would call for military action. If there is an unexpected flare-up on the international scene, they have only to implement the suitable plan.

It is both sensible and practical to have personal contingency plans. When an emergency arises we can fall back on principles and strategies that were drafted when we were not under emotional pressure. The contingency may never happen, but having a plan for that eventuality provides peace of mind and could be a lifesaver.

A common contingency plan is a well designed and rehearsed plan to escape in the event of a fire. A neighbor of mine left a candle burning one night. In the morning he found a smoldering fire in the living room. That experience prodded him to draw up a plan of escape from every room in his large house. He bought needed equipment, and he and his family had periodic fire drills. The plan was spelled out on paper so that it could be reviewed often.

A young missionary couple went to minister in a remote area of Africa. At first the feeling of loneliness haunted them. The wife expressed her qualms about being so isolated by asking, "What would we do if we needed a doctor, or if an accident happened?" To calm her fears the husband asked about the nearest medical facility and any means of available transportation and assistance. He imagined several emergencies that could develop and asked himself, "What would I do in that situation?" He recorded his plans for each emergency in a small notebook which he called *The Emergency Book.* He even specified what should be done about temporary care for the children. All the decisions were made in advance and in great detail.

As time passed those first feelings of isolation and helplessness dissipated. Africa was their home, and they took everything in stride. Then suddenly it happened! The husband was gored by a wild animal. The wife was frantic. What should she do? Then she thought of *The Emergency Book.* It gave her specific instructions for just such an emergency. She handled the crisis with great precision, which contributed greatly to saving her husband's life.

The two contingencies that I have cited anticipate accidents, calamities, and events beyond our control. Another type of plan is also needed in anticipation of a time when our thinking process goes awry. That happens oftener than we like to admit, even to the most brilliant minds. Faulty reasoning produces decisions that often lead to misery.

Emotions are the enemy of clear thinking. A person who is highly emotional in a crisis is intoxicated and doesn't realize it. Surging forces of hatred, love, or fear affect his ability to reason and come to logical conclusions. But how can we anticipate defective thinking? All too often we are not aware of our lapses even when experiencing them.

An obvious solution is to set up a contingency plan to be put in operation in the event an emotional crisis occurs. Do your thinking before you get emotionally involved. Then your decision is made, and all that is necessary is to implement it.

Every person must set up his own contingency plans. What is needful for one is not for another. What one counts as important another may minimize. Establishing a contingency plan is done by envisioning a problem that could develop and then coming to grips with the solution. Face the problem as if it were a current dilemma. Think it through before your emotions are involved. When you have come to a conclusion as to the best course of action, then file your plans for future use. Putting the contingency plan in writing will help you remember it when the crisis occurs.

I have my own personal contingency plans. They take the form of hard and fast rules that I implement when an emergency arises. They bring stability to my life at a time when bewildering moods and overpowering emotions would produce chaos and make it impossible to think clearly. I do not try to impose my plans on others. Neither do I hold myself up as a paragon of virtue in this area. I do think, however, that an example can best convey the truth of an enforced personal discipline. With that in mind may I tell you of three contingency plans which I have had to summon and enforce on a few occasions.

1. *I will not allow any situation to develop
where I won't speak to a person*

The history of the case does not matter. Who is at fault has no bearing on the situation. Whether the other person speaks to me or not doesn't affect my actions. I will put forth an effort to speak regardless of my current feelings. Even when there is an inner hurt, I take myself in hand and put into practice this self-imposed rule of my life.

2. *I will not classify anyone as being my enemy.*

A person may declare war on me. He may talk and act as if he were my enemy. My emotional response may be to retaliate, to classify him as my enemy and thus perpetuate a feud. If I were to make my decision when feelings were running high, there is no question that this is what I would do. Objective thinking, however, produces a different result. Today a person may oppose me on a given issue. Tomorrow he may stand with me and be my friend. Once I classify him as my enemy, he is permanently placed in that category. It is best for me to establish my basic principle when no individual is involved. If tomorrow someone were to declare himself to be my enemy, by word or deed, I would know how to react. I would implement my contingency plan and act accordingly, rather than let powerful emotions and questionable motives tell me what to do.

3. *I will not wrestle with problems in the dark of the night.*

There are times when I awaken at night and cannot go back to sleep. I review recent events, double-check on things I may have forgotten, and formulate my plans for the next day. If there is a problem at hand, or on the horizon, it forces its way into my thinking and crowds out everything else, including the possibility of sleep. I have grappled with both giants and pygmies at such times and always met with defeat. In those dark hours the pygmies themselves look like giants. Things always seem blacker at night, when even the eternal optimist becomes a pessimist. Somehow the nocturnal gloom seeps into the thinking and makes problem solving at that hour a miserable and hopeless task.

I still have wakeful nights, and problems still pound on the door demanding admittance. It is then that I evoke my contingency plan for such an occasion: I refuse to deal with problems until the day has dawned.

In this matter of discipline the spotlight is now on you. You are the trainer and trainee. You set the pattern that will structure your life. Don't be easy on yourself. Draft your contingency plans and then enforce them when the need arises. Lay down the law! Talk to yourself! Exercise dictatorial power! Give crisp orders! Crack the whip!

9

Mastering Our Moods

On the wall of my study are two calibrated instruments. Both are related to the temperature, but their functions are basically different. One is a thermometer and the other is a thermostat. The thermometer registers the temperature, while the thermostat controls it.

Emotions are an integral part of our physical makeup and fluctuate as much as the weather or temperature. They are subjective passions, unanswerable to logic, and they resist any effort to corral them. Like wild horses they run the range at will and are a law unto themselves.

This situation demands a showdown. Just who is in charge in this life of mine? Who calls the shots? Must unstable and mercurial feelings dictate to me? Is it inevitable that I rise and fall with the temperature, or is there a thermostat at my fingertips to provide stability?

Undisciplined emotions have made a shambles of

many lives. When they are allowed to run rampant, energy is wasted, talents are negated, and opportunities are frittered away. A state of blue funk can completely immobilize a person for prolonged periods. Much like children, emotions must be disciplined. Without such restraint, the potential for problems is very great.

Mel is a talented and successful businessman. Yet he has an emotional problem that disrupts his work and home life. He is subject to recurring periods of depression. A cloud comes over his whole personality, and he is sulky, negative, and cantankerous. Then as suddenly as the spell comes, it leaves, and he is his normal, ebullient self again.

When Mel's "mood" hits everything stops. People around him tiptoe around him and bend to his every whim. His family overlooks what he says and makes excuses for him. Secretaries and associates are expected to understand and defer important matters until this trying time passes. It is as if this well-ordered life suddenly surrenders to the dictates of erratic feelings.

Then there is Ted, one of my former subordinates. He is gifted, thorough, and a hard worker. In so many areas he is both qualified and capable. These and other noble traits mark him as one who is bound to succeed.

Yet Ted is anything but a success. He has one trait that has sabotaged all of his good qualities. He is bewilderingly changeable and therefore unreliable.

When Ted accepts a position, he is at first challenged and enthusiastic. He will make this glowing statement, one he has repeated many times: "This is what I've been wanting for so long. I have found my niche. This is my lifework."

Then within a matter of months he is engaged in some other activity and equally excited over it. He wasn't fired from his job but resigned. What causes this changeableness in Ted? When questioned, he frankly states, as if it were a virtue, "I just suddenly felt I wanted to try something else."

Throughout his adult years Ted has been swayed by every gust of feeling that has come his way. When feelings dictate he responds as a dutiful servant. His actions are governed by emotions, and as a result he is inexcusably changeable. Instead of being master of his feelings, they are his master.

When moods are in command, life becomes a roller coaster. To forestall such yo-yo living we can, and must, ride herd on our emotions. That is when self-discipline comes into play. We are compelled to assert our authority and to take charge of our lives. Such a reversal demands resolute determination—but it can be done.

Just what are these moods that vie for control of our lives? To gain mastery over them, we must understand them. Do they have legitimate claims, or are they mere pretenders to the throne?

The basic fact is that moods are feelings: volatile, explosive, unstable, transient feelings. That strips away the aura of glamor. Just because they speak loudly and persistently is no reason to accede to their demands.

Moods have no degree of constancy or consistency. They may come in regular cycles, or they may be erratic and unpredictable. Like geysers, they erupt at unexpected times. They are often triggered by the

slightest of external circumstances or internal conditions. It could be the weather, surrounding conditions,
weariness, grievances (real or imagined), negative
thinking, or a host of other nettlesome provocations.
All these are characteristics of a thermometer, while
what we need is a thermostat.

Respect the Power of Moods

Our emotions are a potent force. At times they are
overpowering. Our feelings can warp our judgment
and impair our ability to think and reason.

Moods fall into two basic categories, the destructive
and the creative. Disruptive and volatile emotions call
for restraint. Bridle them to keep them in check and
don't give up the reins.

A convenient rule of thumb has been borne out by
experience. It has served many well and will do the
same for you. Never make a major decision while in a
destructive mood. Deal with the mood first and then
with the problem.

In grappling with moods, we are not playing with
toys. It is a life-changing struggle with a formidable
foe. The battle will be won. Only you know who the
winner will be.

Harness Your Creative Moods

Helpful, creative moods must be harnessed and put
to work. They are a goading and propelling force. Latch
on to them and use them to your advantage. Start

something when the mood to do so prevails and stay with it as long as the mood lasts.

Refuse to Pamper Your Moods

Our moods are would-be dictators. The more we submit to their demands, the more they expect of us. Unless we break their hammerlock, they will completely dominate us.

Don't jump merely because the candidate for ringmaster cracks the whip. Don't dance to the ever-changing tune of emotions. Don't bow and scrape to morbid moods.

Is the criterion for action determined only by what I feel? Must I do something, or not do it, solely because of an inner sensation? Is anything right or wrong just because of what my emotions say? Kowtowing to moods makes me their slave. The only alternative is to be their master.

Command Your Moods

It is not enough to refuse. We must also choose. Refusing is the negative response, while choosing is the positive one. We must not only learn to say no to the siren song of our moods but also to give distinct commands to them.

The struggle within us is intense. Moods, emotions, and feelings have thrown down the gauntlet. It is a showdown as to who is in control. Assume your rightful position, issue crisp commands, and demonstrate decisively that you are in charge of your own life.

10

The Simple Secret

Years ago a celebrated educator came to a small city to give a lecture. A student was given an assignment to interview him for the school paper.

When the interview was over the young lady closed her notebook and thanked him. Then, almost as an afterthought, she asked, "Is there any bit of advice you can give me as I launch into life?"

Without hesitation he wrote six words on the back of his business card. "Slip this into your purse," he suggested with a smile, "and read it at your leisure."

Those hand-written words of wisdom—LIVE A DAY AT A TIME—proved to be a guiding principle in the kaleidoscopic life and career of Anna Cowper Addison. A host of others have adopted this lifestyle and heartily acclaim its lasting benefits. In her beloved poem, Sybil Partridge sounds the keynote of her life: "Lord, for tomorrow and its needs I do not pray . . . just for today." This classic strategy of living is simple and effective in solving problems. You, too, can use it to great advantage.

When the traumatic experiences of the past and the imagined woes of the future get entangled in our current crises, only confusion and chaos can ensue. It is then that our troubles are compounded beyond measure. Soon the debilitating disease of self-pity rears its ugly head. We may conclude that life is unjust, God is cruel, and everything is stacked against us. The tendency is to lay the blame elsewhere, though much of it belongs at our own doorstep.

In May of 1939 the submarine Squalus had an accident off Hampton Beach, New Hampshire. When the order to submerge was given, one hatch did not close. A torrent of water came rushing in, and the craft plummeted to the bottom. Not all members of the crew were drowned, however. Thirty-three were rescued, due to the quick action of one crewman. All such vessels are made with watertight compartments. When the water came flooding in at one end of the submarine, he quickly slammed the door, saving the lives of those in that part of the vessel.

Life is not just an expanse of time with uncertain boundaries. It is a series of compartments known as days. Each one has its unique joys, challenges, heartaches, and difficulties. With the dawning of each day comes a fresh start and a completely different situation. The key to victorious living is to savor the day's blessings and delights, confront and conquer its problems, and take advantage of its opportunities.

The secret of a happy life is to live a day at a time. Close the door to the troubles of the past. Slam the other door to the worries of the future. Live for today as if there were no other.

Just what have the mistakes of yesterday to do with life today? What possible benefit can come from brooding over past failures? Even constantly reliving prior accomplishments and plaudits is but a way of wasting valuable time and energy. Close the door to keep them from flooding into the compartment of today.

The mystique of the future holds a fascination for many of us. Because it harbors the unknown, a strong curiosity prompts us to pry into it. What we discover is anything but what we need. The future is a hornet's nest of uncertainties, worries, anxieties, cares, fears, and misgivings. These plaques of the future sweep us off our feet. We have enough problems today. Why borrow trouble from tomorrow?

A merciful and considerate God keeps the future veiled. The best thing about the future is that it comes a day at a time. It unfolds to us by degrees and thus enables us to cope with it. What we supposedly see in the future is often only the figment of our imagination. That which looms up so large from the vantage point of today may be only a mirage. The things we dread the most may never happen. What right have the shadowy problems of the future to intrude into life today? Who left the door open to them? Slam both doors, to the past and the future, and live just for today. Jesus clearly summed it up when He said, "Don't worry at all then about tomorrow. Tomorrow can take care of itself! One day's trouble is enough for one day" (Matt. 6:34, PHILLIPS).

One day my friend Perry dropped into my study for a chat. Things were not going well on his job, and he was greatly discouraged.

He began analyzing the reasons for his problems at work. He believed that his troubles began when he chose the wrong major in college. The fact that he was trained in one area but working in another was, in his mind, a great disadvantage. In addition, he had made a faulty decision in his early working days. He felt that many of his fellow workers held this mistake against him, and he couldn't forget it himself.

His most serious handicap, he reasoned, was that he was small of stature. He said that few small men had been successful. When I indicated I couldn't accept his view, he went into a long argument to prove his point. It was as if he wanted it to be so.

This was not a momentary fancy with Perry. I had heard him express these same things often. He kept brooding over them, dragging carcasses out of the past to contaminate the present.

The day wasn't over when I had another visitor. Helen, too, had problems and had to share them with someone. I was the person who would listen and try to help.

Helen had been suffering from insomnia for several weeks. Worries preyed on her mind and robbed her of sleep. Her son, a senior in high school, was not taking his studies as seriously as he should. She envisioned his failure to graduate. With no diploma he would have a difficult time. She was living that trauma as if it had already happened.

Within the past two years both her mother and her

aunt were discovered to be diabetic. Consequently, Helen had been reading everything she could on diabetes. The fact that the disease is often prevalent in entire families didn't help her peace of mind. She even imagined she had some of the symptoms, and the anticipation of what might ensue was making her miserable.

Perry and Helen didn't know each other. Their specific problems were totally unrelated. Yet both of them were borrowing trouble. Perry dredged it out of the past, where it should have remained. Helen snatched hers from a future that might never materialize.

Just why is this concept of living a day at a time so effective? There are two salient reasons. First, experience has proven that even the most gigantic task is easier when broken into segments and dealt with one at a time. I can best develop positive habits by doing so on a daily basis. In the same way, it is easier to break a long-entrenched habit by setting a daily goal. If I vow never again to do something, I assume an awesome and frightening responsibility. But if I conquer a bad habit one day at a time, I am more apt to succeed.

The most important reason for compartmental living is that our strength is allotted on a daily basis. The Bible states, "Your strength will equal your days" (Deut. 33:25, NIV). This same principle is stressed in the prayer Jesus taught His disciples: "Give us each day the bread we need" (Luke 11:3, PHILLIPS). Because our sustenance and strength come in daily quotas, it is only logical that we coordinate our style of living with

God's provision. By living one day at a time, our strength is adequate for our needs.

But what about the time when confusion prevails and our strength seems totally inadequate? Does that nullify the promise? All too often this happens because we do not live a day at a time. Yesterday's difficulties and tomorrow's worries flood into today. The door has been left ajar. The compartment is not watertight. If we use today's quota of energy to relive yesterday and to hassle with tomorrow, it is no wonder that our strength dissipates before we can handle the affairs of today. The load becomes unbearable and we falter. The words of Jesus should continually echo in our ears, "One day's trouble is enough for one day."

Our ration of strength varies with each day. The God who knows us, our needs and our weaknesses, is the dispenser of all strength. He will make sure that our strength meets the requirements of each particular day. His grace is sufficient. The portion is always adequate.

Today is unique and exclusive. The past has been written, the book is closed. There is no guarantee of a tomorrow. Living is for today. The psalmist aptly expressed the joy of living one day at a time: "This is the day the Lord has made; let us rejoice and be glad in it" (Ps. 118:24, NIV).

11

Be a Letter Writer

Writing letters can be either a delightful experience or an unpleasant task. Which is it for you? If you find letter writing difficult, you are certainly not alone. However, do not give up on yourself too easily. The ability to write good letters is a skill that can be learned. All it takes is the diligent application of a few basic principles and, of course, the desire to succeed as a letter writer.

Much has been written on how to write business letters. They are the ones that *must* be written. Other authors have dealt with formal letters that *should* be written. On these pages we will consider only personal letters, ones we *want* to write but often make no more than a feeble attempt at doing so.

Letter writing builds a bridge of friendship that spans the miles. Lord Byron once said, "Letter writing is the only device of combining solitude and good company." In our day it is not the only communication available, but it is one that has distinct advantages.

When one of my sons moved away from home, I made it a point to write him often. On one occasion I phoned him instead. He said, "Thanks, Dad, for the call. But keep those letters coming. I can read them over and over again, and I enjoy them each time."

Letter writing is a skill that must be learned. It is not a divine gift or an innate ability. If you claim that you are just not a letter writer, it is not that you are incapable but that you choose not to learn. The only way to learn to write is by writing.

Now is the time to improve your letter writing. Start today by purchasing a card file (plastic or metal), a package of alphabetical dividers, and one or two packages of 3- × 5-inch cards. This will be your address file. Most people have small address books. A book is more portable, but a file provides much more information and has definite advantages. One advantage is that when there is a change of address the old card can be thrown away and a new one inserted.

Put a name, address, and telephone number on each card. The names and birthdates of the children of the person listed can also be included. Birthdates of growing youngsters can provide an answer when someone asks, "How old is Linda now?" Even the name of the dog will jog your memory. If you have detailed driving instructions to locate the home, then include them also. You probably won't ask for all this information, but when you get it through incoming letters, or in conversation, make sure that it is recorded.

Now comes a very important matter. Put both sides of the card to use. After writing a letter put the date on the reverse side of the card. The next time you write you will know where to begin in reporting events and will avoid needless repetition. If there are further developments you can say, "In my last letter I told you about ———. Since then, ———." You will be surprised how useful that date will be.

You may also want to have a date card tucked away in the back of your file. When something newsworthy happens write the date of the event on this card. Here is an example: *June 16: Trip to Davenport.* If you last wrote on June 7, then you know for certain that you haven't told them about the Davenport trip.

News is the basic ingredient of a good letter. It is what the reader wants to know and what the writer wants to share. The more news a letter contains, the more interesting it is. It may not always be good news but news it is. Anyone who has news to report can not only write a good letter but can also be assured it will be well received.

Conventional news is not letter news. A letter doesn't deal with world affairs, celebrities, or current events. Those are the specialties of the news media.

Letter news is selective and from a limited area. It is mostly personal news from the life, family, and special interests of the writer. Relatives, close friends, and those who know every member of the household will be interested in this information. To others, however, it may be boring. Sometimes it is difficult to remember that detailed news about your in-laws is of little interest to those on your side of the family, unless they know them very well.

Letter news must be carefully selected. On what basis is it chosen? The criterion is very simple. Put yourself in the place of the one to whom you are writing. Will this news be of interest to him? Why? Does it involve someone he knows? Does it pertain to him? If I were living where he is, would I be interested in knowing this? After answering these questions, then make a decision about what to include in the letter.

When considering the above questions, you may think of someone else who would be interested in hearing this news. That may be just enough to prod you to write to another friend.

Many families mail out a general letter at Christmas to all their friends and relatives. It grinds out the experiences of the year for each individual, down to the youngest grandchild. This type of letter isn't personal enough for the closest of friends, and others find little interest in reading about people whom they don't know. Such a letter contains news, but much of it is of little interest to the recipient.

A good letter should have a distinctive slant. It must be personalized at both ends of the line. Let it come from a person and be tailored to another person. Ideally, it should embrace both households. A stock letter, whether duplicated or handwritten, does not serve the purpose. The best letter is born in the heart of the writer and appeals to the interest of the reader.

In a certain small city I know only two persons. One is a cousin and the other is a close friend. Neither one knows the other personally. My friend is rather prominent in the city. When I get a letter from my cousin, he will often enclose a clipping or tell of something which my friend has done recently. The news is of little interest to him, but he knows it is to me. He is thoughtful enough to include this news, which makes his letter that much more interesting.

A newspaper reporter has a nose for news. He is a professional and is ever alert for newsworthy events. Those of us who write letters must also glean the type of news that will make our correspondence stimulating. Our eyes and ears must be ever open for letter news. As we develop such an alertness, it will become as instinctive as it is to a reporter.

During my entire adult life I wrote my mother on a certain day every week and could count on her prompt reply. Throughout the week I jotted down items that would be of interest to her. The list helped greatly in suggesting what to write. Mother has been gone for twenty-five years, but even today I catch myself taking note of news that would be of interest to her.

Some who have an aversion to writing correspond by means of cassette tapes. When the novelty wears off, however, the cost and bother make it more cumbersome than writing. In one home I saw what appeared to be an odd-shaped phone on the kitchen table. I was told it was a tape recorder that the woman used to communicate with her sister. When the microphone was uncradled, the machine was in operation. Instead of taking time to record an entire tape, she did it piecemeal. If she thought of something she wanted to say to her sister, she picked up the microphone and started talking. The success of this method lay in the simplicity and convenience of the tape recorder.

A parallel in conventional correspondence is to take notes when an idea comes. Such reminders should be put in a conspicuous place. If there is an unanswered letter, write it on the back of the envelope. Another way is to clip a scrap of paper to the address card in your file.

Physical endeavor always starts with mental activity. That's where letter writing begins. Don't start cold. Warm up the motor of the mind before putting the hands into gear. Take a little time to think and take notes. Center your thoughts on the person to whom you will be writing. When did you last write? What newsworthy events have happened since then? Who have you seen, or had mail from, recently that he would know? Is there any news about mutual friends? If he were here, what would you tell him?

The best time to write a letter is shortly after receiving one. The channels of communication are open. The ties of friendship have been freshly strengthened. It is as if you've just had a chat with the person. There are questions to be answered and comments to be made about what he has written. Receiving a letter puts you in the mood to reply.

If unanswered letters become a formidable obstacle, then use a little self-conditioning. Lay the bundle of letters on your nightstand. Just before bedtime sort through them and decide which one you will answer the following day. Put the others away, but leave the chosen one in a conspicuous place. Sometimes even addressing the envelope will serve as a reminder. Reading the letter again may provide the breakthrough and get you started.

Always read a letter immediately before answering it. In that way you get the feel of it and can write a better reply. Make a note of all questions asked and anything else that calls for a response. Nothing is more frustrating than to ask a question and to find it has been ignored in the reply. Usually the reason is that the writer did not read the letter before writing.

When corresponding regularly with an individual, set a certain day for writing. Choose the day that will fit into your schedule and suggest that the other party do the same. Having such a schedule, and sticking to it, makes letter writing easier and more enjoyable.

Although news is the "meat and potatoes" of a letter, it is not the whole meal. A good letter writer, like a good cook, adds a garnish to make the fare more palatable. Variety itself creates and maintains interest. Season the staple food with a dash of humor, a pithy quote, a pertinent observation, or a gracious compliment.

A letter need not be a literary work of art. The content is far more important than the construction. Forget the antiquated phrases of the past and write as you talk. Express yourself in the way that comes naturally. Let your personality permeate what you write and radiate to the reader. Your letter will be effective if the reader senses that you are writing to him as if you were having a friendly chat.

No one enjoys getting mail more than I do. I'll go even a step further. No one enjoys writing letters more than I do. With that background, let me give my choice of the most delightful letter to receive and the most enjoyable to write.

The most delightful letter to receive is the one that comes as a complete surprise. The writer is usually someone I know well but from whom I have never received a letter. No pressing need prompts it, and no urgent request is involved. The person acts on a sudden impulse, and his letter is warm and friendly. It expresses appreciation for a friendship spanning the years and undiminished by intervening distances. Such a letter makes my day, and I bask in its afterglow.

My choice for the most enjoyable letter to write is, again, the surprise letter. I have learned to respond to certain sudden, but gentle, impulses. If I ignore them they vanish as quickly as they came. Out of nowhere may come a desire to write a certain person. There is no demanding reason to do so and no penalty if I don't. It is just a feeling that surfaces momentarily, and I do something about it right then. I have a chat with the friend by means of a letter. I share news, express appreciation, encourage, and compliment. From the outset I explain that the letter does not necessarily call for a reply. Often a heartwarming reply does come, but this is a bonus. The real compensation came earlier through the gratifying experience of writing a surprise letter.

This is not a textbook, and I am not a schoolmaster. Yet the time has come for an assignment. Right now I want you to write a surprise letter. My purpose is not to burden you with a difficult task but to lead you into a joyful experience.

To whom will this letter be written? The choice is yours. You may decide to write to someone with a prolonged illness, an aged couple forgotten in the whirl of life, a teacher who greatly influenced you, the one who helped you through college, one you have secretly admired, or someone who is greatly discouraged.

Now is the time. Close this book and start. Put forth your very best efforts. Make the letter warm, friendly, and newsy. Then send it on its way.

I predict this will be a rewarding experience—the first of many for you.

Happy letter writing!

12

Time for Sale

Time is the basic substance of life. It is God's gift to us, and yet it can be purchased or bartered. Like money, it can be squandered, spent wisely, or invested for future dividends. It is a limited commodity, but it is not scarce. Every person is given an equal daily allotment of time, but still some have more at their disposal than others.

Does this all sound contradictory? Can these paradoxical statements be true? Perhaps a further exploration of the subject will provide the answer.

The Bible, which is a very practical book, says, "Make the best use of your time" (Eph. 5:16, PHILLIPS). Another translation adds a pungent line, "Like sensible men, not like simpletons" (NEB). The King James Version uses the phrase "redeeming the time." This is the language of the marketplace and means "buying time."

There is at least one area in which we are all equal.

Each day contains 24 hours, or 1,440 minutes. It is the same for the rich or the poor, the educated or the illiterate, the winner or the loser. In spite of the uniform allotment of time, some people accomplish much more than others. The secret is, of course, in how time is used.

We treat few things more illogically than time. We covet it like misers and waste it like spendthrifts. We feel frustrated because we do not have more time, yet we squander it lavishly. Lucius Seneca, a Roman philosopher, sagely observed, "We are always complaining that our days are few and at the same time acting as if they would never end."

Five simple organizational secrets can provide additional time for you. They will not only make you more productive and efficient but will also go a long way toward dispelling the frustrations that plague an ambitious person. With just a little effort these secrets can become part of your busy life.

Plan Your Time

At the beginning of each day, list the tasks that need to be done. Establish priorities and then do the most important job first.

Give priority to the creative work facing you and leave the routine items until later in the day. It is also wise to earmark the chore you dread the most and face it head-on by doing it first, or at least early in the day. Postponing a dreaded task will tend to make it seem insurmountable. The prolonged period of anxiety will become a horrible frustration.

If every item on your list has been scratched by the end of the day, you will experience a delightful sense of accomplishment. If not, then put the remaining entries on the next day's list—in order of priority. You must determine whether it is more effective to complete your designated undertakings each day or to have a long list and continually work at whittling it down.

Buy Time

How can you buy time when no more is available? We hear about saving time, but can it really be purchased? Actually all of us buy time, whether we realize it or not. With careful planning we can buy even more.

I buy time from the telephone company each month. In exchange for the small amount I pay, they make it unnecessary for me to run time-consuming errands or to travel great distances to converse with another person. When I hire someone to mow my lawn or wash my car, I pay a small sum and in exchange I have time to do more important work. If I am not pressed for time, then I can do the chores myself and save a little money. Many similar decisions confront me. Shall I be my own mechanic or take my car to a shop? Shall I paint the house or hire someone? Shall I cut wood for the fireplace or buy it from a dealer? It all depends on which is more valuable for the moment, my time or my money.

There is an old story from the days when trains were means of transportation. A minister walked into a coach and sat down beside another gentleman. In the course of their conversation he discovered that the

other man was also a preacher. They had a long, interesting conversation as they shared their experiences in
the ministry. Finally, one stood up to leave.

"I must get back to the Pullman," he said. "I imagine
the porter has my berth made up by now."

"I never take a sleeper," replied his fellow pastor in a
critical tone of voice. "I'm saving God's money."

"Well, I'm saving God's man," came the quick retort.

Too often we think only of saving money. It is
possible to be penny wise and pound foolish. Shall we
save money and squander time and energy? Or is there
a better way? We must budget our time as well as our
funds. Remember, however, that you *can* buy time.

Invest Time

Money can be spent, or it can be invested. The same
is true of time. To invest time is to use it in such a way
as to bring future benefits. Invested time brings an
abundant harvest in years to come.

I have made great use of a typewriter all of my adult
life. That doesn't mean that I have been a good typist
all that time, however. I started off with an old Oliver
typewriter that didn't even have a standard keyboard.
I used the Columbus system—discover a key and then
land on it. My friends were amazed at my speed, but
my accuracy left much to be desired.

One day I purchased a Remington noiseless portable.
With it came a little book telling how to learn the touch
system of typing. There were also a few exercises. I
kept the Oliver and did my work and correspondence

on it. I never used the new machine except when practicing the touch system. I set aside one hour a day for my typing lesson and stayed with it conscientiously. After two months I junked the Oliver and have been a good typist ever since. I invested sixty hours in learning to type. Who can calculate the time I have saved in the forty-two years since that time?

My friend Anton is an executive for a large corporation. When the art of speed reading was just emerging, he became captivated by its potential. He bought a book that spelled out the principles of speed reading and worked diligently at learning to read faster. Later he took a night course in speed reading. His friends laughed at him. They said it was a fad and could even be harmful to the eyes. Some intimated that he had been suckered out of both his money and his time. Over the years Anton has learned to read at a remarkable rate. His skill has helped him to keep abreast of things in the world. He also attributes his consistent promotions at work to his well-developed reading ability. The small amount of time and money invested has paid great dividends.

Ed is a pastor of a large city congregation. He started out, however, in a small country church in the Blue Ridge Mountains of Virginia. Because he had comparatively little to do in those days, he spent much of his time studying and organizing his library. Over the years his efforts have paid off magnificently. Now, when the demands on his time are great, his study is so organized that he can find information on almost any subject within two minutes. The time he invested while in that first church has helped him to save time in every other church he has served.

Invested dollars pay back in multiplied dollars when they are needed. Invested time pays back in kind, many times multiplied, at a period in life when it may be a scarce commodity.

Set Priorities

There is not enough time to do everything you want to do. Once you face that fact you must decide the degree of importance of each job. By establishing priorities you can use the limited time available to the best purposes.

One subtle danger is to establish a work pattern in which we get bogged down in enjoyable tasks at the expense of far more important matters. In such instances the priority is based on our own enjoyment rather than actual importance.

A case in point is the avid sports fan. He could easily devote all his reading time to books and magazines about his athletic heroes. But enjoyment is not the exclusive criterion in establishing priorities. One must weigh all factors and not let an enjoyable activity eliminate a necessary one.

Many times I have been so weighed down with tasks and responsibilities that I felt completely swamped. I have learned to cope with that situation by organizing my jobs on a priority basis. Instead of letting a mob of tasks surround and trample me to death, I force them into single file and handle them one at a time. If I tackle the biggest job first, each succeeding one becomes easier.

Delegate Responsibilities

To delegate is to share responsibilities with your subordinates. The art of delegation requires: 1) entrusting responsibilities to others, 2) allowing them freedom to make decisions, and 3) exercising great restraint in second-guessing their decisions. An oft-repeated axiom is, "The test of a leader is not what he can do himself but in what he can inspire [and in some instances *permit*] others to do."

Delegation is not easy. It goes against the very nature of an ambitious person. The more talented a person is, the harder it is for him to delegate responsibilities to others. It is often easier to do a job himself than to get another to do it.

President Theodore Roosevelt colorfully expressed the importance of delegating when he said, "The best executive is one who has sense enough to pick good men to help him and self-restraint enough to keep from meddling with them while they do it." The person who can truly delegate authority and fully entrust responsibility to others has learned one of the greatest secrets of success. And anyone who wishes to manage his time well *must* learn to delegate.

A young secretary saw a book on my desk titled *Help Yourself to Time*. Because she seemed interested, I suggested that she take it home to read. A few days later she returned, bubbling over with enthusiasm.

"Would you permit me to loan this book to my boss?" she asked. "If anyone needs it, he does."

I encouraged her to do so. The next day she returned, a bit crestfallen. It seems that she had gone into her boss's office and, with characteristic enthusiasm, told him about the book and how much it had helped her.

"Would you like to read it before I return it to my friend?" she asked.

He scanned the index and leafed through the pages.

"Yes, that looks very good," he intoned, "but I just don't have the time to read it."

Time is the essence of life. It is God's gift to us. Use it wisely and it will serve you well.

13

How to Remember

The mind of man is the most wonderful instrument ever created. God gave us the power of perception, reasoning, and memory. We tend to take these capabilities for granted until calamity snatches them from us.

Every aspect of the mind is intriguing, but one of the most valuable, and the most neglected, is memory. We accept the fact that a baby is given a mind and must develop it as he grows, but too often we count memory as being a complete package that can neither develop nor deteriorate. In this we make a grave mistake.

All knowledge rests on the basic foundation of memory. Without the ability to recall past accomplishments or previously learned facts, there can be no further progress. Memory can be likened to a savings account into which deposits are made and from which they are later withdrawn.

Perhaps a more graphic picture would be to compare memory to a vast filing cabinet. Whether or not we can summon information at will is often determined by our filing system. Events and facts that fall helter-skelter into the storehouse of memory soon get buried under the debris of the past. They are there, but finding them is next to impossible. A good file clerk can find any document or letter at will because he adheres to a few simple rules of filing. The same is true of the filing cabinet of the memory. Understanding how the memory works, and the principles of recalling information, helps greatly in the time of need.

"The average man does not use 10 percent of his actual inherited capacity for memory," said psychologist Carl Seashore. "He wastes 90 percent by violating the laws of memory." An inadequately functioning memory is more the result of neglect than any other contributing factor.

The average person sabotages his own memory. He does so by adopting one of two faulty attitudes. The first attitude is exemplified by the person who says, "My memory is poor, and there is nothing I can do about it." The other extreme is the person who says, "I have a good memory. What more do I want?" The first type of person believes his memory cannot be improved, and the second feels his need not be. Both are radically wrong, and by their attitudes are severely curtailing their own abilities.

There is no such thing as a good or bad memory. One person may be very adept in storing and recalling certain kinds of information but absolutely useless in retaining other kinds. The one who has a phenomenal storehouse of names may not be able to remember figures.

In his heyday, James A. Farley, Postmaster General under President Franklin D. Roosevelt, could recall the first names of ten thousand men. Toscanini, the Italian conductor, could direct entire symphonies without referring to a music score. It is probable that Farley's memory was poor on music and Toscanini's weak on names.

It is not uncommon for a contractor to have dimensions and measurements on the tip of his tongue, while the sports fan can recite the batting averages of every player on his favorite team. Usually a person's memory is best on a subject in which he is vitally interested.

The sum and substance of our education is not what we have studied but what we have retained. Our knowledge is not measured by the books we have read or the degrees we have earned, but by how much information is readily available to us through our memory's filing system.

Since memory is such an important factor in our lives, it is peculiar that more effort is not made to improve it. Schools urge us to remember, tell us what to remember, but give absolutely no instruction as to how to do so. In this area formal education fails. Just a little time spent in studying the basic laws of memory, in learning why we remember, and why we forget, will improve our productivity and efficiency in many areas of our lives.

One of the popular fallacies that discourages the development of memory is the belief that the mind has a limited capacity. Some individuals claim they are exercising discrimination in what they file away in their memory. Their reasoning is that they do not want to take up important space with trivia. This reasoning is faulty because it misrepresents the human mind. There are no specific boundaries to the capacity of man's memory. It is not limited by the number of cubic inches in the cranial cavity nor is there a finite number of file cabinets which will eventually be filled to overflowing. Learning to remember relatively unimportant items only strengthens the ability to remember the more important ones.

"The memory strengthens as you lay burdens upon it and becomes trustworthy as you trust it," said Thomas DeQuincy, the English essayist. Just as you exercise and develop your muscles to become proficient in physical feats, so you can develop your memory. Muscles that are unused become weak and useless. The same is true of the mind, and of memory in particular.

Developing the memory can be a challenging and enjoyable pursuit. It can be undertaken alone or with other members of the family. The group enterprise, approached with the goal of having fun, can enhance the memory of every participant, no matter what his walk in life.

An alert, retentive memory is one of life's greatest assets. A dull and undeveloped one is more than an annoyance; it is a severe handicap. Sharpness of memory is not the result of heredity so much as it is of adherence to the principles of remembering. A sluggish memory can be helped by consciously practicing a few simple rules.

The art of improving the efficiency of the memory is called mnemonics. Volumes have been written on the subject, but the basic principles of mnemonics can be summarized in four key words.

Intention

The first step in remembering is determining to do so. Basically, we remember what we want to remember and forget what we want to forget. Thorndike's law of effect says we tend to recall those experiences which give us pleasure and avoid those which give us pain. We can remember what we count as important but find it difficult to recall what we think is unimportant.

Every one of us has had an experience that illustrates this truth. Perhaps you were visiting a strange city. Your host traversed a certain route from his office to his home. You had been seemingly alert as you rode along. But if you were asked to drive back to the office, you wouldn't have the faintest idea how to get there. It is not that the route was complicated or that you don't have the ability to remember. The truth is that you didn't anticipate the need to know the route. You didn't intend to remember the directions or the various turns. Had you known you would be required to find your way back, remembering the route would have been simple.

Dr. Alfred Adler, the noted Viennese psychologist, once wrote, "The experiences a person easily recalls give us important clues as to his personality." In general, the person recalls those things that he considers important.

Even an artificial interest in a subject is better than no interest at all. Some who have had no motive for remembering certain facts develop a motive by cultivating an interest in the subject.

During the early years of the television quiz shows, Dr. Joyce Brothers won a large sum of money by answering questions in the field of professional boxing. She recalled facts and figures from the pugilistic world with an ease that was astounding. Later she told the full story. Dr. Brothers was a student of mnemonics and could qualify as a memory expert. (She is co-author of the book *Ten Days to a Successful Memory.*) Seeing the huge sums of money being given away, she determined she would win some of it. The statistics and records on boxing are compact and readily available. They provided a comparatively simple challenge to her ability to commit facts to memory. The result of her efforts soon became known to television viewers throughout the nation. Her interest in boxing was slight, but, with a monetary motive, she developed an artificial interest in the subject.

The basis of all learning is motivation. Thus, a fundamental rule for remembering is to develop a motive to do so.

Attention

A faulty memory is not so much a matter of forgetting as it is of not "getting" in the first place. "I feel there is no such thing as ultimate forgetting," wrote Thomas DeQuincy. "Traces once impressed upon the memory are indestructible." There is much evidence to the effect that we never completely forget what we have thoroughly learned.

Thomas A. Edison once said, "The average person's brain does not observe one-thousandth part of what his eye observes." Too often the things that we see do not register. Views, experiences, and facts flow like a mountain stream through our thinking channels, but only little eddies and pools remain.

If vital information is to be recalled at will, then we must take time to file it in the archives of the memory. In giving undivided attention to the material, we go a long way toward seeing that it will not be forgotten.

Understanding

We tend to remember best not only what we are most interested in, but also what we understand best. Memorizing a paragraph from a scientific paper is next to impossible if you do not understand what the author is attempting to express. Remembering the details of a doctor's prescription is hopeless if the terms are foreign to you.

The clearer the meaning, the easier it is to remember. Fully comprehending the meaning and significance of the facts is an aid to memory.

Association

The mind is an associating machine. The basis of all memory is in the association of ideas, facts, and experiences. To understand the principle of association, and to learn to make use of it, is to have a key to a vast storehouse of knowledge.

Filing information in the memory is similar to the

work of a bricklayer. He connects the bricks with mortar. In a similar way we connect new ideas with ones that are well established. Any thought entering the mind without being associated with a previous thought will soon be lost.

We form associations either consciously or unconsciously. From childhood we have been associating instinctively. By consciously working at the art of association, we can greatly improve our ability to remember.

A natural association is, of course, the best; but if one is not available, then we must invent one. This can be done in a variety of ways, depending on our ingenuity and imagination. Mental cartooning and caricature can make an idea so distinctive that it will never be lost. Even a weak association is better than none at all.

Over two thousand years ago Aristotle first stated three laws of association.

The first is the *law of resemblance.* Words that have a similar sound or meaning are naturally linked together. For instance, *sympathy* and *empathy.*

The second is the *law of contrasts.* Impressions that are exact opposites tend to call the other extreme to mind. For instance, *white—black* and *hot—cold.* By linking ideas with their opposites we have a means of calling them to mind.

The third law of association is the *law of contiguity.* A simpler expression would be to call it the principle of togetherness. When things are usually linked together, the mention of one will often bring the other to mind. The word *ham* is quickly associated with *eggs.* The name

Punch brings to mind *Judy*. This law would also cover things that happen at the same time.

Each of us uses these principles of association. By being consciously aware of them, we can develop our memory into a more effective tool.

14

Your Life Story

It is a prudent person who jots down observations about the events and experiences of his life. Such a record is of inestimable value and grows in value with the passing years.

In the past it was very common for individuals to keep lengthy journals. Colonial pioneers, frontiersmen, statesmen, and educators were compelled to write of their activities. Religious leaders such as Luther, Wesley, and Whitefield recorded their spiritual conflicts, opinions, and feelings. Much of the material for the biographies of these men came from their journals. It is entirely possible that they never realized the wealth of material they were leaving for posterity when they took time to write what were just the routine happenings of their lives.

The simplest way to keep personal experiences and recollections alive is by means of a diary. It is not only an aid to memory but an ever-increasing storehouse of dates, events, names, places, and other useful information. The effort expended is minimal and the benefits manifold. In later years the sheer joy of reading and reminiscing makes the hurried scribblings priceless.

A diary is a daily register of events, handwritten and usually in book form. The entries can be fairly long or very brief. Sentences can be written in full or with just enough words to convey the information. Often symbols and abbreviations are used to conserve space. A diary is a personal record, and each person must determine what character the writing assumes.

A typical diary contains one 4- × 5½-inch page for each day in the year. Usually there is a choice of a one-year diary or a five-year one. In the one-year diary the whole page is used for the day's entry. In the five-year diary there are five spaces on the page, and each year on a particular date a short entry is made in one of the spaces.

Most people will find the five-year diary more suitable to their needs. It is better to make brief entries consistently than to become too ambitious and then bog down completely.

I started with a five-year diary thirty-nine years ago and have stayed with it. By writing small I can make a fifty-word entry in the allotted space. Of course there are days when I could write much more, but usually the space is adequate.

Before buying your diary you may want to conduct an experiment. Write fifty words on the events of the day. Then use three hundred words to report on the same day. How much space do you really need? How much would you need on an average day? After answering these questions you will be better able to make your decision.

There is one appealing advantage to the five-year diary: the entries of the previous years are directly above the new entries. It is interesting to read what happened exactly one, two, three, or four years ago on the same date as your present entry.

Just what should go into a diary? Because a diary is a personal record of events, experiences, observations, and feelings, you should write whatever seems important to you. Even general news can be related to your personal life. Recently I had occasion to read my entry for March 28, 1969. It stated, "Ex-President Eisenhower died today. I don't know when I have felt the loss of a public figure so keenly." Not only was this a news item, but it was also linked to my feelings.

The more factual information you put in your diary, the more valuable it will become. Once you start including names, places, and other details, your diary will become a personal source book.

In my travels I have been the guest of hundreds of persons who were previously unknown to me. Often we were together for only a meal. If I have so much as a snack with someone, in a restaurant or a home, their name goes into my diary. If Bart Betterman drives me to the airport, his name will appear in my diary. If his son Bobby rides along, I will take note of that also. This information may prove to be invaluable when I return to the area.

Diaries provide fascinating reading. Some time ago, my wife and I started reading aloud from my very first diary. We were amazed at how much we had forgotten.

It was great fun reliving past experiences, sometimes shedding a tear but more often howling with laughter. We've even let others in on the fun. When close friends visit we read aloud from the times we were together in the past. Those diaries are more interesting than any books we have ever read.

You will probably never have your biography written, nor is it likely that a publisher will solicit your autobiography. Yet it is possible to have the story of your life in several bound volumes.

Now is the time to begin the first segment of your life story.

15

Resources Galore

Absolute self-sufficiency is a myth. Each of us has limitations. Sooner or later every individual comes to the end of his tether and reaches out for help. Psychiatrists and counselors so often hear the same opening remark: "I never dreamed I would appeal to anyone for help—but here I am."

In the previous chapters I have stressed self-discipline as a way to structure our lives. I would be remiss to overlook those occasions when a helping hand is needed.

I never cease to be amazed at the ability of those in the legal profession. There are thousands of laws and court cases, and attorneys are expected to know them all. When chatting with a lawyer friend I expressed my wonder at all the information he has on the tip of his tongue. I have never forgotten his reply. "Attorneys don't have all the answers," he said, "but they do know where they can be found. They don't always have them on the tip of their tongues, but they do have them at their fingertips."

Fred retired after spending all of his working years in an office. The first year the relaxed life was wonderful. He caught up on the many little things that needed to be done around his home and did a lot of reading. But he soon became restless, and time began to hang heavy on his hands. Both he and his wife agreed that he must find some kind of work to occupy his time.

Fred had always been fairly good as a handyman. Esther reminded him of all the householders who need help along that line. He decided to get a few more tools and become a professional handyman. He put an ad in the paper and eagerly awaited the response.

The first job was only three blocks away and lasted just two hours. Fred came home greatly elated. This was going to be a breeze. When the second call came, he went to check it out. To his dismay, it was a difficult job that he had never done before. Fear and panic gripped him. His first reaction was to make an excuse and bow out. But he surprised himself by saying, "I can get to it on Thursday morning."

That afternoon Fred went to the city library. There he found a complete encyclopedia giving detailed instructions for many types of repair work. There were also volumes that dealt with the very problem that he was now facing. He read the material and made notes. Thursday morning he started the job with the confidence of a veteran. He's been doing repair work ever since and has been a great success. The library proved to be a valuable resource for Fred's second career.

Twenty-five years ago, a young, inexperienced woman named Eppie Lederer found herself competing against twenty-eight professionals. The prize—a post as writer of an advice-to-the-lovelorn column in the Chicago Sun-Times. Each aspirant was given a set of difficult questions sent in by readers. While the others tried to answer the questions from their own experience, Eppie consulted the "experts." Today, she is still answering questions and giving advice under the name of Ann Landers.

Those first answers bore the trait that has become the hallmark of her column. Ann knew she did not have all the answers, so she turned to the authorities who did have them. If the question was on a legal matter, she consulted her friend Justice William O. Douglas. If it pertained to the Catholic Church, she consulted Father Theodore Hesburgh, president of Notre Dame University. In fielding difficult questions Ann still refers to her expert consultants and often mentions them by name. Even the advisor to millions does not have all the answers, but she knows where she can get them.

Don't hoodwink yourself into thinking that you are self-sufficient. The most gifted persons are inadequate at times, and even the most resourceful must enlist the aid of others. It is no disgrace to need, or ask for, help. Accepting the fact that you need help is a mark of maturity. At such a time one relinquishes the role of bluffer and learns to seek and accept help graciously.

To compensate for our deficiencies, we have boundless resources. The secret is in knowing just where and how to tap them. It is not essential to know everything.

The key is to be able to find what we need to know when we need it.

Extensive information, on almost any subject, is available in the public library. The library is a gold mine of valuable data to those who are willing to do a little prospecting. Reference books contain helpful material in condensed form and also tell where additional information on a particular subject can be found. Attendants will assist in finding material on any given subject. They will also explain how to use the card file of books or the "Readers Guide to Periodical Literature."

Many libraries participate in the interlibrary loan system. If yours is one of them, you can obtain books from many of the largest libraries in the nation. Even the Library of Congress is a part of this system. There is a nominal fee for the service, usually the cost of postage and insurance.

Another source of information is the counsel, advice, and guidance that comes from others. To tap such resources we must be perceptive enough to acknowledge our need, sensible enough to seek help, and humble enough to take the advice that we receive.

First, there is what is often called professional help, which includes persons who are highly trained in special areas and who will share their knowledge and expertise for a fee. Lawyers, physicians, certified public accountants, psychiatrists, psychologists, and a variety of consultants open a wide door of help in time of need.

Most guidance, however, can be had for the asking. In fact, there is so much free advice floating around that we must be very choosy. Much of it is impractical, faulty, and calls for careful evaluation. The ability to select the best advice is a mark of maturity.

There are two types of extremists in this matter. One takes advice from no one and the other takes advice from everyone. Both demonstrate a lack of wisdom and stand only to lose.

Be selective in choosing your advisors. Often those who volunteer and are the most profuse with their counsel are the least qualified to give it. Remember the old saying: "Don't buy hair restorer from a bald-headed barber." Don't seek advice from a pauper on making money. Don't ask about the path to success from the glib talker who is a failure. Don't seek help in practical living from a theorist who lives in an ivory tower.

A strange disease afflicts humans during the teen years. It is seldom fatal but can be very debilitating. Thus far no cure has been found for this malady, nor is there a prescription that will combat the symptoms. The only hopeful thing is that eventually each person outgrows the disease, although it takes much longer in some cases than others. Were I to give you the technical name for the disease, you would not recognize it. You will identify it, however, when I describe the basic symptom. The young person in the grip of this sickness will take advice from no one except his peers. He believes that anyone older, no matter how experienced, successful, or gifted, doesn't know what he is talking about. All the answers must come from fellow adolescents. Most of us have come out of this illness alive and should have learned a lesson from it.

During the sixties an axiom was born and voiced by the young demonstrators. They kept reminding themselves, "Don't trust anyone over thirty." Then, oh so quickly, they entered that third decade of life and were haunted by their glib advice.

What a storehouse of wise counsel is available to us! We can pick and choose the persons who will mold our lives. Seek out and cherish the best of advice. Listen attentively to the successful, the wise and experienced, the ignorant and the novice. Let your advisors be those who embody the idea of your own aspirations.

When considering our extensive resources, we must not overlook the greatest one of all. The omnipotent God, who rules the universe, is personally and vitally interested in each of us.

Jesus clearly expressed God's concern for us. "Are not five sparrows sold for two pennies? Yet not one of them is forgotten by God. Indeed, the very hairs of your head are all numbered. Don't be afraid; you are worth more than many sparrows" (Luke 12:6, 7, NIV). "Consider how the lillies grow. They do not labor or spin. Yet I tell you, not even Solomon in all his splendor was dressed like one of these. If that is how God clothes the grass of the field, which is here today, and tomorrow is thrown into the fire, how much more will he clothe you, O you of little faith!" (Luke 12:27, 28, NIV).

The God who is so concerned for our welfare repeatedly reminds us of what is available for just the asking. "If any of you lacks wisdom, he should ask God, who gives generously to all, without finding fault, and it will be given to him" (James 1:5, NIV). Another promise opens a wide door to us: "Call to me and I will answer you and tell you great and unsearchable things you do not know" (Jer. 33:3, NIV).

When every resource is exhausted God's reservoir is undiminished. When all human help fails He still extends His strong arm and says, "You do not have, because you do not ask God" (James 4:2, NIV).

Postscript

Don't Always Believe Your Friends

You can't always believe what even your closest friends say.

My friend, Bruce, has been bald since he was twenty. Many bald men are self-conscious about their condition, but not Bruce. In fact, he has capitalized on his shiny pate. He is a gifted public speaker and has an inexhaustible repertoire of humorous stories about baldness. He invariably begins his speeches with one of those stories and thus establishes an immediate rapport with his audience.

One day I was in a counseling session with Bruce. Out of the blue he exclaimed, "What bugs me the most is that I don't have a beautiful shock of curly hair."

I would have never guessed that Bruce was sensitive about his baldness. I doubt if any of his many friends even suspect it. When I expressed my surprise he said,

"Oh, that joking is a defense mechanism. I laugh at myself before the other fellow gets a chance to comment about it. If he does get the first shot, I've always got a good comeback. But it still hurts."

Shortly after that, I had an experience that helped me understand Bruce's behavior. While attending a large national convention, my nose became inflamed. It was embarrassing, to say the least. People started asking about it, and I instinctively took the offensive. When someone started talking to me, I would launch into my spiel: "Boy, I'm going to have to swear off drinking Pepsi Cola. Look what it has done to my nose." My humor, like that of Bruce's, was a facade to hide my chagrin.

Bruce and I are not alone in this matter. Others also compensate for their insecurities with quips, humor, and other verbal parries. Even bragging often stems from insecurity.

Many people use this same tactic when defending their lifestyles. They laugh and joke about how unstructured their lives are. They even exaggerate to make their stories more humorous. To hear them talk you would almost think they were proud of their uncoordinated and disorganized lifestyles.

These people may appear to be bragging, but, in fact, they are confessing. They are hurting, and the outward show is just a defense mechanism. They sing the praises of a happy-go-lucky life while yearning for a coordinated and efficient one.

Bruce compensated with humor because he could not grow luxuriant hair. I did the same because I could do nothing about my inflamed nose. Had we been able to resolve our predicaments, we would have done so.

The problem of unstructured living is entirely different. There is a solution. Efficiency, planning, and organization are within the reach of everyone.

Your cluttered life can be organized. But only one person can do it. That person is you. The ball is in your court.

You *can* manage your life!